OCCULT PHILOSOPHY OR MAGICK - NATURAL MAGIC

Occult Philosophy or Magick - Natural Magic

Henry Cornelius Agrippa

Contents

1	Section 1	1
2	Section 2	25
3	Section 3	45
4	Section 4	61
5	Section 5	77
6	Section 6	101
7	Section 7	135

1

Section 1

Chap. i. How Magicians Collect vertues from the three-fold World, is declared in these three Books.

Seeing there is a three-fold World, Elementary, Celestiall, and Intellectual, and every inferior is governed by its superior, and receiveth the influence of the vertues thereof, so that the very original, and chief Worker of all doth by Angels, the Heavens, Stars, Elements, Animals, Plants, Metals, and Stones convey from himself the vertues of his Omnipotency upon us, for whose service he made, and created all these things: Wise men conceive it no way irrationall that it should be possible for us to ascend by the same degrees through each World, to the same very originall World it self, the Maker of all things, and first Cause, from whence all things are, and proceed; and also to enjoy not only these vertues, which are already in the more excellent kind of things, but also besides these, to draw new vertues from above. Hence it is that they seek after the vertues of the Elementary world, through the help of Physick [=medicine], and Naturall Philosophy in the various mixtions of Naturall things, then of the Celestiall world in the Rayes, and influences thereof, according to the rules of Astrologers, and the doctrines of Mathematicians, joyning the Celestiall vertues to the former: Moreover, they ratifie and confirm all these with the powers of divers Intelligences, through the sacred Ceremonies of Religions. The order and process of all these I shall endeavor to deliver in these three Books: Whereof the forst contains naturall Magick, the second Celestiall, and the third Ceremoniall. But I know not whether it be an unpardonable presumption in me, that I, a man of so little judgement and learning, should in my very youth so confidently set upon a business so difficult, so hard, and intricate as this is. Wherefore, whatsoever things have here already, and shall afterward be said by me, I would not have any one assent to them, nor shall I my self, any further then they shall be approved of by the Universall Church, and the Congregation of the Faithfull.

Chap. ii. What Magick is, What are the Parts thereof, and how the Professors thereof must be Qualified.

Magick is a faculty of wonderfull vertue, full of most high mysteries, containing the most profound Contemplation of most secret things, together with the nature, power, quality, substance, and vertues thereof, as also the knowledge of whole nature, and it doth instruct us concerning the differing, and agreement of things amongst themselves, whence it produceth its wonderfull effects, by uniting the vertues of things through the application of them one to the other, and to their inferior sutable subjects, joyning and knitting them together thoroughly by the powers, and vertues of the superior Bodies. This is the most perfect and chief Science, that sacred and sublimer kind of Phylosophy [philosophy], and lastly the most absolute perfection of all most excellent Philosophy. For seeing that all regulative Philosophy is divided into Naturall, Mathematicall, and Theologicall: (Naturall Philosophy teacheth the nature of those things which are in the world, searching and enquiring into their Causes, Effects, Times, Places, Fashions, Events, their Whole, and Parts, also

The Number and the Nature of those things,
Cal'd Elements, what Fire, Earth, Aire forth brings: From whence the Heavens their beginnings had; Whence Tide, whence Rainbow, in gay colours clad. What makes the Clouds that gathered are, and black,

To send forth Lightnings, and a Thundring crack; What doth the Nightly Flames, and Comets make; What makes the Earth to swell, and then to quake:

What is the seed of Metals, and of Gold

What Vertues, Wealth, doth Nature's Coffer hold.

All these things doth naturall Philosophy, the viewer of nature contain, teaching us according to Virgil's Muse.

- Whence all things flow,

Whence Mankind, Beast; whence Fire, whence Rain, and Snow,

Whence Earth-quakes are; why the whole Ocean beats

Over his Banks, and then again retreats;

Whence strength of Hearbs [herbs], whence Courage, rage of Bruits [brutes],

All kinds of Stone, of Creeping things, and Fruits.

But Mathematicall Philosophy teacheth us to know the quantity of naturall Bodies, as extended into three dimensions, as also to conceive of the motion, and course of Celestiall Bodies.

- As in great hast [haste],

What makes the golden Stars to march so fast; What makes the Moon sometimes to mask her face, The Sun also, as if in some disgrace.

And as Virgil sings,

How th' Sun doth rule with twelve Zodiack Signs, The Orb thats measur'd round about with Lines, It doth the Heavens Starry way make known, And strange Eclipses of the Sun, and Moon.

Arcturus also, and the Stars of Rain,

The Seaven Stars likewise, and Charles his Wain, Why Winter Suns make tow'rds the West so fast; What makes the Nights so long ere they be past?

All which is understood by Mathematicall Philosophy.

- Hence by the Heavens we may foreknow

The seasons all; times for to reap and sow, And when 'tis fit to launch into the deep,

And when to War, and when in peace to sleep, And when to dig up Trees, and them again

To set; that so they may bring forth amain.

Now Theologicall Philosophy, or Divinity, teacheth what God is, what the Mind, what an Intelligence, what an Angel, what a Divell [devil], what the Soul, what Religion, what sacred Institutions, Rites, Temples, Observations, and sacred Mysteries are: It instructs us also concerning Faith, Miracles, the vertues of Words and Figures, the secret operations and mysteries of Seals, and as Apuleius saith, it teacheth us rightly to understand, and to be skilled in the Ceremoniall Laws, the equity of Holy things and rule of Religions. But to recollect my self) these three principall faculties Magick comprehends, unites, and actuates; deservedly therefore was it by the Ancients esteemed as the highest, and most sacred Philosophy. It was, as we find, brought to light by most sage Authours [authors], and most famous Writers; amongst which principally Zamolxis and Zoroaster were so famous, that many believed they were the inventors of this Science. Their track [footsteps] Abbaris the Hyperborean, Charmondas, Damigeron, Eudoxus, Hermippus followed: there were also other eminent, choice men, as Mercurius Tresmegistus [Trismegistus], Porphyrius [Porphyry], Iamblicus [Iamblichus], Plotinus, Proclus, Dardanus, Orpheus the Thracian, Gog the Grecian, Germa the Babilonian [Babylonian], Apollonius of Tyana, Osthanes also wrote excellently in this Art; whose Books being as it were lost, Democritus of Abdera recovered, and set forth with his own Commentaries.

Besides Pythagoras, Empedocles, Democritus, Plato, and many other renowned Philosophers travelled far by Sea to learn this Art: and being returned, published it with wonderfull devoutness, esteeming of it as a great secret. Also it is well known that Pythagoras, and Plato went to the Prophets of Memphis to learn it, and travelled through almost all Syria, Egypt, Judea, and the Schools of the Caldeans [Chaldaeans], that they might not be ignorant of the most sacred Memorials, and Records of Magick, as also that they might be furnished with

Divine things. Whosoever therefore is desirous to study in this Faculty, if he be not skilled in naturall Philosophy, wherein are discovered the qualities of things, and in which are found the occult properties of every Being, and if he be not skilful in the Mathematicks, and in the Aspects, and Figures of the Stars, upon which depends the sublime vertue, and property of every thing; and if he be not learned in Theologie [theology], wherein are manifested those immateriall substances, which dispence [dispense], and minister all things, he cannot be possibly able to understand the rationality of Magick. For there is no work that is done by meer Magick, nor any work that is meerly Magicall, that doth not comprehend these three Faculties.

Chap. iii. Of the four Elements, their qualities, and mutuall mixtions.

There are four Elements, and originall grounds of all corporeall things, Fire, Earth, Water, Aire, of which all elementated inferiour bodies are compounded; not by way of heaping them up together, but by transmutation, and union; and when they are destroyed, they are resolved into Elements. For there is none of the sensible Elements that is pure, but they are more or less mixed, and apt to be changed one into the other: Even as Earth becoming dirty, and being dissolved, becomes Water, and the same being made thick and hard, becometh Earth again; but being evaporated through heat, passeth into Aire, and that being kindled, passeth into Fire, and this being extinguished, returns back again into Aire, but being cooled again after its burning, becometh Earth, or Stone, or Sulphur, and this is manifested by Lightening [lightning]: Plato also was of that opinion, that Earth was wholly changeable, and that the rest of the Elements are changed, as into this, so into one another successively. But it is the opinion of the subtiller sort of Philosophers, that Earth is not changed, but relented and mixed with other Elements, which do dissolve it, and that it returns back into it self again. Now, every one of the Elements hath two specificall qualities, the former whereof it retains as proper to it self, in the other, as a mean, it agrees with that which comes next after it. For Fire is hot and dry, the Earth dry and cold, the Water cold and moist, the Aire moist and ot. And so after this manner the Elements, according to two contrary qualities, are contrary one to the other, as Fire to Water, and Earth to Aire. Moreover, the Elements are upon another account opposite one to the other: For some are heavy, as Earth and Water, and others are light, as Aire and Fire. Wherefore the Stoicks called the former passives, but the latter actives. And yet once again Plato distinguished them after another manner, and assigns to every one of them three qualities, viz. to the Fire brightness, thinness and motion, but to the Earth darkness, thickness and quietness. And according to these qualities the Elements of Fire and Earth are contrary. But the other Elements borrow their qualities from these, so that the Aire receives two qualities of the Fire, thinness and motion; and one of the Earth, viz. darkness. In like manner Water receives two qualities of the Earth, darkness and thickness, and one of Fire, viz. motion. But Fire is twice more thin then Aire, thrice more movable, and four times more bright: and the Aire is twice more bright, thrice more thin, and four times more moveable then Water. Wherefore Water is twice more bright then Earth, thrice more thin, and four times more movable. As therefore the Fire is to the Aire, so Aire is to the Water, and Water to the Earth; and again, as the Earth is to the Water, so is the Water to the Aire, and the Aire to the Fire. And this is the root and foundation of all bodies, natures, vertues, and wonderfull works; and he which shall know these qualities of the Elements, and their mixtions, shall easily bring to pass such things that are wonderfull, and astonishing, and shall be perfect in Magick.

Chap. iv. Of a three-fold consideration of the Elements.
There are then, as we have said, four Elements, without the perfect knowledge whereof we can effect nothing in Magick. Now each of them is three-fold, that so the number of four may make up the num-

ber of twelve; and by passing by the number of seven into the number of ten, there may be a progress to the supream Unity, upon which all vertue and wonderfull operation depends. Of the first Order are the pure Elements, which are neither compounded nor changed, nor admit of mixtion, but are incorruptible, and not of which, but through which the vertues of all naturall things are brought forth into act. No man is able to declare their vertues, because they can do all things upon all things. He which is ignorant of these, shall never be able to bring to pass any wonderfull matter. Of the second Order are Elements that are compounded, changeable, and impure, yet such as may by art be reduced to their pure simplicity, whose vertue, when they are thus reduced to their simplicity, doth above all things perfect all occult, and common operations of nature: and these are the foundation of the whole naturall Magick. Of the third Order are those Elements, which originally and of themselves are not Elements, but are twice compounded, various, and changeable one into the other. They are the infallible Medium, and therefore are called the middle nature, or Soul of the middle nature: Very few there are that understand the deep mysteries thereof. In them is, by means of certain numbers, degrees, and orders, the perfection of every effect in what thing soever, whether Naturall, Celestiall, or Supercelestiall; they are full of wonders, and mysteries, and are operative, as in Magick Naturall, so Divine: For from these, through them, proceed the bindings, loosings, and transmutations of all things, the knowing and foretelling of things to come, also the driving forth of evil, and the gaining of good spirits. Let no man, therefore, without these three sorts of Elements, and the knowledge thereof, be confident that he is able to work any thing in the occult Sciences of Magick, and Nature. But whosoever shall know how to reduce those of one Order, into those of another, impure into pure, compounded into simple, and shall know how to understand distinctly the nature, vertue, and power of them in number, degrees, and order, without dividing the substance, he shall easily attain to the knowledge, and perfect operation of all Naturall things, and Celestiall secrets.

Chap. v. Of the wonderfull Natures of Fire, and Earth.
There are two things (saith Hermes) viz. Fire and Earth, which are sufficient for the operation of all wonderfull things: the former is active, the latter passive. Fire (as saith Dionysius) in all things, and through all things, comes and goes away bright, it is in all things bright, and at the same time occult, and unknown; When it is by it self (no other matter coming to it, in which it should manifest its proper action) it is boundless, and invisible, of it self sufficient for every action that is proper to it, moveable, yielding it self after a maner to all things that come next to it, renewing, guarding nature, enlightening, not comprehended by lights that are vailed [veiled] over, clear, parted, leaping back, bending upwards, quick in motion, high, alwayes raising motions, comprehending another, not Comprehended it self, not standing in need of another, secretly increasing of it self, and manifesting its greatness to things that receive it; Active, Powerfull, Invisibly present in all things at once; it will not be affronted or opposed, but as it were in a way of revenge, it will reduce on a sudden things into obedience to it self; incomprehensible, impalpable, not lessened, most rich in all disensations of it self. Fire (as saith Pliny) is the boundless, and mischievous part of the nature of things, it being a question whether it destroys, or produceth most things. Fire it self is one, and penetrates through all things (as say the Pythagorians) also spread abroad in the Heavens, and shining: but in the infernall place streightened, dark, and tormenting, in the mid way it partakes of both. Fire therefore in it self is one, but in that which receives it, manifold, and in differing subjects it is distributed in a different manner, as Cleanthes witnesseth in Cicero. That fire then, which we use is fetched out of other things. It is in stones, and is fetched out by the stroke of the steele; it is in Earth, and makes that, after digging up, to smoake [smoke]: it is in Water, and heats springs, and wells: it is in

the depth of the Sea, and makes that, being tossed with winds, warm: it is in the Aire, and makes it (as we oftentimes see) to burn.

And all Animals, and living things whatsoever, as also all Vegetables are preserved by heat: and every thing that lives, lives by reason of the inclosed heat. The properties of the Fire that is above, are heat, making all things Fruitfull, and light, giving life to all things. The properties of the infernall Fire are a parching heat, consuming all things, and darkness, making all things barren. The Celestiall, and bright Fire drives away spirits of darkness; also this our Fire made with Wood drives away the same, in as much as it hath an Analogy with, and is the vehiculum of that Superior light; as also of him, who saith, I am the Light of the World, which is true Fire, the Father of lights, from whom every good thing that is given, Comes; sending forth the light of his Fire, and communicating it first to the Sun, and the rest of the Celestiall bodies, and by these, as by mediating instruments, conveying that light into our Fire. As, therefore the spirits of darkness are stronger in the dark: so good spirits, which are Angels of Light, are augmented, not only by that light, which is Divine, of the Sun, and Celestiall, but also by the light of our common Fire. Hence it was that the first, and most wise institutors of Religions, and Ceremonies ordained, that Prayers, Singings, and all manner of Divine Worships whatsoever should not be performed without lighted Candles, or Torches. (Hence also was that significant saying of Pythagoras, Do not speak of God without a Light) and they commanded that for the driving away of wicked spirits, Lights and Fires should be kindled by the Corpses of the dead, and that they should not be removed untill the expiations were after a Holy manner performed, and they buried. And the great Jehovah himself in the old Law Commanded that all his Sacrifices should be offered with Fire, and that Fire should always be burning upon the Altar, which Custome the Priests of the Altar did always observe, and keep amongst the Romanes. Now the Basis, and foundation of all the Elements, is the Earth, for that is the object, subject, and receptacle of all Celestiall rayes, and influencies;

in it are contained the seeds, and Seminall vertues of all things; and therefore it is said to be Animall, Vegetable, and Minerall. It being made fruitfull by the other Elements, and the Heavens, brings forth all things of it self; It receives the abundance of all things, and is, as it were the first fountain, from whence all things spring, it is the Center, foundation, and mother of all things. Take as much of it as you please, seperated, washed, depurated, subtilized, if you let it lye [lie] in the open Aire a little while, it will, being full, and abounding with Heavenly vertues, of it self bring forth Plants, Worms, and other living things, also Stones, and bright sparks of Metals. In it are great secrets, if at any time it shall be purified by the help of Fire, and reduced unto its simplicity by a convenient washing. It is the first matter of our Creation, and the truest Medicine that can restore, and preserve us.

Chap. vi. Of the wonderfull Natures of Water, Aire, and Winds. The other two Elements, viz. Water, and Aire, are not less efficacious then the former; neither is nature wanting to work wonderfull things in them. There is so great a necessity of Water, that without it no living thing can live. No Hearb [herb], nor Plant whatsoever, without the moistening of Water can branch forth. In it is the Seminary vertue of all things, especially of Animals, whose seed is manifestly waterish. The seeds also of Trees, and Plants, although they are earthy, must notwithstanding of necessity be rotted in Water, before they can be fruitfull; whether they be imbibed with the moisture of the Earth, or with Dew, or Rain, or any other Water that is on purpose put to them. For Moses writes, that only Earth, and Water bring forth a living soul. But he ascribes a twofold production of things to Water, viz. of things swimming in the Waters, and of things flying in the Aire above the Earth. And that those productions that are made in, and upon the Earth, are partly attributed to the very Water, the same Scripture testifies, where it saith that the Plants, and the Hearbs [herbs] did not grow, because God had not caused it to rain upon the Earth. Such is the efficacy of this Element of Water, that Spirituall regeneration cannot be done without it, as Christ himself testified to Nicodemus. Very great also is the vertue of it in the Religious Worship of God, in expiations, and purifications; yea, the necessity of it is no less then that of Fire. Infinite are the benefits, and divers are the uses thereof, as being that by vertue of which all things subsist, are generated, nourished and increased. Thence it was that Thales of Miletus, and Hesiod concluded that Water was the beginning of all things, and said it was the first of all the Elements, and the most potent, and that because it hath the mastery over all the rest. For, as Pliny saith, Waters swallow up the Earth, extinguish flames, ascend on high, and by the stretching forth of the clouds, challenge the Heaven for their own: the same falling become the Cause of all things that grow in the Earth. Very many are the wonders that are done by Waters, according to the Writings of Pliny, Solinus, and many other Historians, of the wonderfull vertue whereof, Ovid also makes mention in these Verses.

- Hornd Hammons Waters at high noon

Are cold; hot at Sun-rise and setting Sun. Wood, put in bub'ling Athemas is Fir'd,

The Moon then farthest from the Sun retir'd; Circonian streams congeal his guts to Stone That thereof drinks, and what therein is thrown. Crathis and Sybaris (from the Mountains rol'd) Color the hair like Amber or pure Gold.

Some fountains, of a more prodigious kinde, Not only change the body but the minde.

Who hath not heard of obscene Salmacis? Of th' Æthiopian lake? for, who of this

But only tast [taste], their wits no longer keep, Or forthwith fall into a deadly sleep.

Who at Clitorius fountain thirst remove, Loath Wine, and abstinent, meer Water love.

With streams oppos'd to these Lincestus flowes:

They reel, as drunk, who drink too much of those. A Lake in fair Ar-

cadia stands, of old
Call'd Pheneus; suspected, as twofold:
Fear, and forbear to drink thereof by night:
By night unwholesome, wholesome by day-light.

Josephus also makes relation of the wonderfull nature of a certain river betwixt Arcea, and Raphanea, Cities of Syria: which runs with a full Channell all the Sabboth [Sabbath] Day, and then on a sudden ceaseth, as if the springs were stopped, and all the six dayes you may pass over it dry-shod: but again, on the seaventh day (no man knowing the reason of it) the Waters return again in abundance, as before. Wherefore the inhabitants thereabout called it the Sabboth-day river, because of the Seaventh day, which was holy to the Jews. The Gospel also testifies to a sheep-pool, into which whosoever stepped first, after the Water was troubled by the Angel, was made whole of whatsoever disease he had. The same vertue, and efficacy we read was in a spring of the Ionian Nymphs, which was in the territories belonging to the Town of Elis, at a Village called Heraclea, neer the river Citheron: which whosoever stepped into, being diseased, came forth whole, and cured of all his diseases. Pausanias also reports, that in Lyceus, a mountain of Arcadia, there was a spring called Agria, to which, as often as the dryness of the Region threatned [threatened] the destruction of fruits, Jupiters Priest of Lyceus went, and after the offering of Sacrifices, devoutly praying to the Waters of the Spring, holding a Bough of an Oke [oak] in his hand, put it down to the bottome of the hallowed Spring; Then the waters being troubled, a Vapour ascending from thence into the Air was blown into Clouds, with which being joyned together, the whole Heaven was overspread: which being a little after dissolved into rain, watered all the Country most wholsomly [wholesomely]. Moreover Ruffus a Physitian [physician] of Ephesus, besides many other Authours, wrote strange things concerning the wonders of Waters, which, for ought I know, are found in no other Authour.

It remains that I speak of the Aire. This is a vitall spirit, passing through all Beings, giving life, and subsistence to all things, binding, moving, and filling all things. Hence it is that the Hebrew Doctors reckon it not amongst the Elements, but count it as a Medium or glew [glue], joyning things together, and as the resounding spirit of the worlds instrument. It immediately receives into it self the influences of all Celestiall bodies, and then communicates them to the other Elements, as also to all mixt [mixed] bodies: Also it receives into it self, as it were a divine Looking-glass, the species of all things, as well naturall, as artificiall, as also of all manner of speeches, and retains them; And carrying them with it, and entering into the bodies of Men, and other Animals, through their pores, makes an Impression upon them, as well when they sleep, as when they be awake, and affords matter for divers strange Dreams and Divinations. Hence they say it is, that a man passing by a place where a man was slain, or the Carkase [carcass] newly hid, is moved with fear and dread; because the Aire in that place being full of the dreadfull species of Man-slaughter [manslaughter], doth, being breathed in, move and trouble the spirit of the man with the like species, whence it is that be comes to be afraid. For every thing that makes a sudden impression, astonisheth nature. Whence it is, that many Philosophers were of opinion that Aire is the cause of dreams, and of many other impressions of the mind, through the prolonging of Images, or similitudes, or species (which are fallen from things and speeches, multiplyed in the very Aire) untill they come to the senses, and then to the phantasy, and soul of him that receives them, which being freed from cares, and no way hindred, expecting to meet such kind of species, is informed by them. For the species of things, although of their own proper nature they are carryed to the senses of men, and other animals in generall, may notwithstanding get some impression from the Heaven, whilest they be in the Aire, by reason of which, together with the aptness and disposition of him that receives them, they may be carryed to the sence [sense] of one rather then of another. And hence it is possible naturally, and far from all manner of superstition, no other spirit coming between, that a man should be able in a very time to signifie his mind unto another man, abiding at a very long and unknown distance from him; although he cannot precisely give an estimate of the time when it is, yet of necessity it must be within 24 hours; and I my self know how to do it, and have often done it. The same also in time past did the Abbot Tritemius [Trithemius] both know and do. Also, when certain appearances, not only spirituall, but also naturall do flow forth from things, that is to say, by a certain kind of flowings forth of bodies from bodies, and do gather strength in the Air, they offer, and shew themselves to us as well through light as motion, as well to the sight as to other senses, and sometimes work wonderfull things upon us, as Plotinus proves and teacheth. And we see how by the South wind the Air is condensed into thin clouds, in which, as in a Looking-glass are reflected representations at a great distance of Castles, Mountains, Horses, and Men, and other things, which when the clouds are gone, presently vanish. And Aristotle in his Meteors shews, that a Rainbow is conceived in a cloud of the Aire, as in a Looking-glass. And Albertus saith, that the effigies of bodies may by the strength of nature, in a moist Aire be easily represented, in the same manner as the representations of things are in things. And Aristotle tels of a man, to whom it happened by reason of the weakness of his sight, that the Aire that was near to him, became as it were a Looking-glass to him, and the optick beam did relect back upon himself, and could not penetrate the Aire, so that whithersoever he went, he thought he saw his own image, with his face towards him, go before him. In like manner, by the artificialnes of some certain Looking-glasses, may be produced at a distance in the Aire, beside the Looking-glasses, what images we please; which when ignorant men see, they think they see the appearances of spirits, or souls; when indeed they are nothing else but semblances kin to themselves, and without life. And it is well known, if in a dark place where there is no light but by the coming in of a beam of the sun somewhere through a litle hole, a white paper, or plain

Looking-glass be set up against that light, that there may be seen upon them, whatsoever things are done without, being shined upon by the Sun.

And there is another sleight, or trick yet more wonderfull. If any one shall take images artificially painted, or written letters, and in a clear night set them against the beams of the full Moon, whose re-semblances being multiplyed in the Aire, and caught upward, and reflected back together with the beams of the Moon, any other man that is privy to the thing, at a long distance sees, reads, and knows them in the very compass, and Circle of the Moon, which Art of declaring secrets is indeed very profitable for Towns, and Cities that are besieged, being a thing which Pythagoras long since did often do, and which is not unknown to some in these dayes, I will not except my self. And all these, and many more, and greater then these, are grounded in the very nature of the Aire, and have their reasons, and causes declared in Mathematicks, and Opticks. And as these resemblances are reflected back to the sight, so also sometimes to the hearing, as is manifest in the Echo. But there are more secret arts then these, and such whereby any one may at a very remote distance hear, and understand what another speaks, or whispers softly.

There are also from the airy Element Winds. For they are nothing else, but Air moved and stirred up. Of these there are four that are principall, blowing from the four corners of the Heaven, viz. Notus from the South, Boreas from the North, Zephyrus from the West, Eurus from the East, which Pontanus comprehending in these verses, saith,

Cold Boreas from the top of 'lympus [Olympus] blows, And from the bottom cloudy Notus flows.
From setting Phoebus fruitfull Zeph'rus flies, And barren Eurus from the Suns up-rise.

Notus is the Southern Wind, cloudy, moist, warm, and sickly, which Hieronimus cals the butler of the rains. Ovid describes it thus,

Out flies South-wind, with dropping wings, who shrouds His fearful aspect in the pitchie clouds,

His white Haire stream's, his Beard big-swoln with showres [showers]; Mists binde his Brows, rain from his Bosome powres [pours].

But Boreas is contrary to Notus, and is the Northern Wind, fierce, and roaring, and discussing clouds, makes the Aire serene, and binds the Water with Frost. Him doth Ovid thus bring in speaking of himself.

Force me befits: with this thick cloud I drive;

Toss the blew Billows, knotty Okes [oaks] up-rive; Congeal soft Snow, and beat the Earth with haile; When I my brethren in the Aire assaile,

(For thats our Field) we meet with such a shock, That thundring Skies with our encounters rock

And cloud-struck lightning flashes from on high, When through the Crannies of the Earth I flie,

And force her in her hollow Caves, I make

The Ghosts to tremble, and the ground to quake.

And Zephyrus, which is the Western Wind, is most soft, blowing from the West with a pleasant gale, it is cold and moist, removing the effects of Winter, bringing forth Branches, and Flowers. To this Eurus is contrary, which is the Eastern wind, and is called Apeliotes; it is waterish, cloudy, and ravenous. Of these two Ovid sings thus:

To Persis and Sabea, Eurus flies;

Whose gums perfume the blushing Mornes up-rise:

Next to the Evening, and the Coast that glows With setting Phoebus, flowry Zeph'rus blows:

In Scythia horrid Boreas holds his rain, Beneath Boites, and the frozen Wain:

The land to this oppos'd doth Auster steep

With fruitfull showres, and clouds which ever weep.

Chap. vii. Of the kinds of Compounds, what relation they stand in to the Elements, and what relation there is betwixt the Elements themselves, and the soul, senses, and dispositions of men.

Next after the four simple Elements follow the four kinds of perfect Bodies compounded of them, and they are Stones, Metals, Plants, and Animals: and although unto the generation of each of these all the Elements meet together in the composition, yet every one of them follows, and resembles one of the Elements, which is most predominant. For all Stones are earthy, for they are naturally heavy, and descend, and so hardened with dryness, that they cannot be melted. But Metals are waterish, and may be melted, which Naturalists confess, and Chymists [chemists] finde to be true, viz. that they are generated of a viscous Water, or waterish argent vive. Plants have such an affinity with the Aire, that unless they be abroad in the open Aire, they do neither bud, nor increase. So also all Animals

Have in their Natures a most fiery force, And also spring from a Celestiall source.

And Fire is so naturall to them, that that being extinguished they presently dye [die]. And again every one of those kinds is distinguished within it self by reason of degrees of the Elements. For amongst the Stones they especially are called earthy that are dark, and more heavy; and those waterish, which are transparent, and are compacted of water, as Crystall, Beryll, and Pearls in the shels [shells] of Fishes: and they are called airy, which swim upon the Water, and are spongious [spongeous], as the Stones of a Sponge, the pumice Stone, and the Stone Sophus: and they are called fiery, out of which fire is extracted, or which are resolved into Fire, or which are produced of Fire: as Thunderbolts, Fire-stones, and the Stone Asbestus [asbestos]. Also amongst Metals, Lead, and Silver are earthy; Quicksilver is waterish: Copper, and Tin are airy: and Gold, and Iron are fiery. In Plants also, the roots resemble the Earth, by reason of their thickness: and the leaves, Water, because of their juice: Flowers, the

Aire, because of their subtility, and the Seeds the Fire, by reason of their multiplying spirit. Besides, they are called some hot, wine cold, sonic moist, some dry, borrowing their names from the qualifies of the Elements. Amongst Animals also, some are in comparison of others earthy, and dwell in the bowels of the Earth, as Worms and Moles, and many other small creeping Vermine; others are watery, as Fishes; others airy, which cannot live out of the Aire: others also are fiery, living in the Fire, as Salamanders, and Crickets, such as are of a fiery heat, as Pigeons, Estriches [ostriches], Lions, and such as the wise man cals beasts breathing Fire. Besides, in Animals the Bones resemble the Earth, Flesh the Aire, the vital spirit the Fire, and the humors the Water. And these humors also partake of the Elements, for yellow choller [choler] is instead of Fire, blood instead of Aire, Flegme [phlegm] instead of Water, and black choller [choler], or melancholy instead of Earth.

And lastly, in the Soul it self, according to Austin [Augustine], the understanding resembles Fire, reason the Aire, imagination the Water, and the senses the Earth. And these senses also are divided amongst themselves by reason of the Elements, for the sight is fiery, neither can it perceive without Fire, and Light: the hearing is airy, for a sound is made by the striking of the Aire; The smell, and tast [taste] resemble the Water, without the moisture of which there is neither smell, nor tast [taste]; and lastly the feeling is wholly earthy, and taketh gross bodies for its object. The actions also, and the operations of man are governed by the Elements. The Earth signifies a slow, and firm motion; The water signifies fearfulness, & sluggishness, and remisseness in working: Aire signifies chearfulness [cheerfulness], and an amiable disposition: but Fire a fierce, quick and angry disposition. The Elements therefore are the first of all things, and all things are of, and according to them, and they are in all things, and diffuse their vertues through all things.

Chap. viii. How the Elements are in the Heavens, in Stars, in Divels [devils], in Angels, and lastly in God himself.

It is the unanimous consent of all Platonists, that as in the originall, and exemplary World, all things are in all; so also in this corporeal world, all things are in all; so also the Elements are not only in these inferior bodies, but also in the Heavens, in Stars, in Divels [devils], in Angels, and lastly in God, the maker and originall example of all things. Now in these inferiour bodies the Elements are accompanied with much gross matter; but in the Heavens the Elements are with their natures, and vertues, viz. after a Celestiall, and more excellent manner, then in sublunary things. For the firmness of the Celestiall Earth is there without the grossness of Water: and the agility of the Aire without running over its bounds; the heat of Fire without burning, only shining, and giving life to all things by its heat. Amongst the Stars, also, some are fiery, as Mars, and Sol; airy, as Jupiter, and Venus: watery, as Saturn, and Mercury: and earthy, such as inhabit the eighth Orbe, and the Moon (which notwithstanding by many is accounted watery) seeing, as if it were Earth, it attracts to it self the Celestiall waters, with which being imbibed, it doth by reason of its neerness [nearness] to us power [pour] out, and communicate to us. There are also amongst the signes, some fiery, some earthy, some airy, some watery: the Elements rule them also in the Heavens, distributing to them these four threefold considerations Of every Element, viz. the beginning, middle, and end: so Aries possesseth the beginning of Fire, Leo the progress, and increase, and Sagittarius the end. Taurus the beginning of the Earth, Virgo the progress, Capricorn the end. Gemini the beginning of the Aire, Libra the progress, Aquarius the end. Cancer the beginning of Water, Scorpius [Scorpio] the middle, and Pisces the end. Of the mixtions therefore of these Planets and Signes, together with the Elements are all bodies made. Moreover Divels [devils] also are upon this account distinguished the one from the other, so that some are called fiery, some earthy, some airy, and some watery. Hence also those four Infernall Rivers, fiery Phlegethon, airy Cocytus, watery Styx, earthy Acheron. Also in the Gospel we read of Hell Fire, and eternall Fire, into which the Cursed shall be commanded to go: and in the Revelation we read of a Lake of Fire, and Isaiah speaks of the damned, that the Lord will smite them with corrupt Aire. And in Job, They shall skip from the Waters of the Snow to extremity of heat, and in the same we read, That the Earth is dark, and covered with the darkness of death, and miserable darkness. Moreover also these Elements are placed in the Angels in Heaven, and the blessed Intelligencies; there is in them a stability of their essence, which is an earthly vertue, in which is the stedfast seat of God; also their mercy, and piety is a watery cleansing vertue. Hence by the Psalmist they are called Waters, where he speaking of the Heavens, saith, Who rulest the Waters that are higher then the Heavens [Ps148.4;] also in them their subtill [subtle] breath is Aire, and their love is shining Fire. Hence they are called in Scripture the Wings of the Wind; and in another place the Psalmist speaks of them, Who makest Angels thy Spirits, and thy Ministers a flaming fire. Also according to orders of Angels, some are fiery, as Seraphin [Seraphim], and authorities, and powers; earthy as Cherubin [Cherubim]; watery as Thrones, and Archangels: airy as Dominions, and Principalities. Do we not also read of the original maker of all things, that the earth shall he opened and bring forth a Saviour? Is it not spoken of the same, that he shall be a fountain of living Water, cleansing and regenerating? Is not the same Spirit breathing the breath of life; and the same according to Moses, and Pauls testimony, A consuming Fire? That Elements therefore are to be found every where, and in all things after their manner, no man can deny: First in these inferiour bodies feculent and gross, and in Celestials more pure, and clear; but in supercelestials living, and in all respects blessed. Elements therefore in the exemplary world are Idea's of things to be produced, in Intelligencies are distributed powers, in Heavens are vertues, and in inferiour bodies gross forms.

Chap. ix. Of the vertues of things Naturall, depending immediatly upon Elements.

Of the naturall vertues of things, some are Elementary, as to heat, to cool, to moisten, to dry; and they are called operations, or first qualities, and the second act: for these qualities only do wholly change the whole substance, which none of the other qualities can do. And some are in things compounded of Elements, and these are more then first qualities, and such are those that are maturating, digesting, resolving, mollifying, hardening, restringing, absterging, corroding, burning, opening, evaporating, strengthening, mitigating, conglutinating, obstructing, expelling, retaining, attracting, repercussing, stupifying [stupefying], bestowing, lubrifying, and many more. Elementary qualities do many things in a mixt [mixed] body, which they cannot do in the Elements themselves. And these operations are called secondary qualities, because they follow the nature, and proportion of the mixtion of the first vertues, as largely it is treated of in Physick [Medical] Books. As maturation, which is the operation of naturall heat, according to a certain proportion in the substance of the matter. Induration is the operation of cold; so also is congelation, and so of the rest. And these operations sometimes act upon a certain member, as such which provoke Urine, Milk, the Menstrua, and they are called third qualities, which follow the second, as the second do the first.

According therefore to these first, second, and third qualities many diseases are both cured, and caused. Many things also there are artificially made, which men much wonder at; as is Fire, which burns Water, which they call the Greek Fire, of which Aristotle teacheth many compositions in his particular Treatise of this subject. In like manner there is made a Fire that is extinguished with Oyl [oil], and is kindled with cold Water, when it is sprinkled upon it; and a Fire which is kindled either with Rain, Wind, or the Sun; and there is made a Fire, which is called burning Water, the Confection whereof is well known, and it consumes nothing but it self: and also there are made Fires that cannot be quenched, and incombustible Oyles [oils], and perpetuall Lamps, which can be extinguished neither with Wind, nor

Water, nor any other way; which seems utterly incredible, but that there had been such a most famous Lamp, which once did shine in the Temple of Venus, in which the stone Asbestos did burn, which being once fired can never be extinguished. Also on the contrary, Wood, or any other combustible matter may be so ordered, that it can receive no harm from the Fire; and there are made certain Confections, with which the hands being anointed, we may carry red hot Iron in them, or put them into melted Metall, or go with our whole bodies, being first anointed therewith, into the Fire without any manner of harm, and such like things as these may be done.

There is also a kind of flax, which Pliny calls Asbestum, the Greeks call Ασβεζον, which is not consumed by Fire, of which Anaxilaus saith, that a Tree compassed about with it, may be cut down with insensible blows, that cannot be heard.

Chap. x. Of the Occult Vertues of things.

There are also other vertues in things, which are not from any Element, as to expell poyson [poison], to drive away the noxious vapours of Minerals, to attract Iron, or any thing else; and these vertues are a sequell of the species, and form of this or that thing; whence also they being little in quantity, are of great efficacy; which is not granted to any Elementary quality. For these vertues having much form, and litle matter, can do very much; but an Elementary vertue, because it hath more materiality, requires much matter for its acting. And they are called occult qualities, because their Causes lie hid, and mans intellect cannot in any way reach, and find them out. Wherefore Philosophers have attained to the greatest part of them by long experience, rather then by the search of reason: for as in the Stomack [stomach] the meat is digested by heat, which we know; so it is changed by a certain hidden vertue which we know not: for truly it is not changed by heat, because then it should rather be changed by the Fire side, then in the Stomack [stomach]. So there are in things, besides the Elementary qualities which we know, other certain imbred vertues created by nature, which we admire, and are amazed at, being such as we know not, and indeed seldom or never have seen. As we read in Ovid of the Phoenix, one only Bird, which renews her self.

All Birds from others do derive their birth, But yet one Fowle there is in all the Earth, Call'd by th' Assyrians Phoenix, who the wain Of age, repairs, and sows her self again.

And in another place,

Ægyptus came to see this wondrous sight:
And this rare Bird is welcom'd with delight.

Long since Metreas [Matreas] brought a very great wonderment upon the Greeks, and Romans concerning himself. He said that he nourished, and bred a beast that did devour it self. Hence many to this day are solicitous, what this beast of Matreas should be. Who would not wonder that Fishes should be digged out of the Earth, of which Aristotle, Theophrastus, and Polybius the Historian makes mention? And those things which Pausanius wrote concerning the singing Stones? All these are effects of occult vertues.

So the Estrich [ostrich] concocts cold, and most hard Iron, and digests it into nourishment for his body; whose Stomack [stomach] they also report, cannot be hurt with red hot Iron. So that little Fish called Echeneis doth so curb the violence of the Winds, and appease the rage of the Sea, that, let the Tempests be never so imperious, and raging, the Sails also bearing a full Gale, it doth notwithstanding by its meer touch stay the Ships, and makes them stand still, that by no means they can be moved. So Salamanders, and Crickets live in the Fire; although they seem sometimes to burn, yet they are not hurt. The like is said of a kind of Bitumen, with which the weapons of the Amazons were said to be smeared over, by which means they could be spoiled neither with Sword nor Fire; with which also the Gates of Caspia, made of Brass, are reported to be smeared over by Alexander the great. We read also that Noah's Ark was joyned together with this Bitumen, and that it endured some thousands of years upon the Mountains of Armenia. There are many such kind of wonderfull things, scarce credible, which notwithstanding are known by experience. Amongst which Antiquity makes mention of Satyrs, which were Animals, in shape half men, and half bruits [brutes], yet capable of speech, and reason; one whereof S. Hierome reporteth, spake once unto holy Antonius the Hermite, and condemned the errour of the Gentiles, in worshipping such poor creatures as they were, and desired him that he would pray unto the true God for him; also he affirms that there was one of them shewed openly alive, and afterwards sent to Constantine the Emperour.

2

Section 2

Chap. xi. How Occult Vertues are infused into the severall kinds of things by Idea's, through the help of the Soul of the World, and rayes of the Stars: and what things abound most with this Vertue. Platonists say that all inferiour bodies are exemplified by the superiour Ideas. Now they define an Idea to be a form, above bodies, souls, minds, and to be one, simple, pure, immutable, indivisible, incorporeal, and eternall: and that the nature of all Idea's is the same. Now they place Idea's in the first place in very goodness it self (i.e.) God, by way of cause; and that they are distinguished amongst themselves by some relative considerations only, least whatsoever is in the world, should be but one thing without any variety, and that they agree in essence, least God should be a compound substance. In the second place, they place them in the very intelligible it self (i.e.) in the Soul of the world, differing the one from the other by absolute forms, so that all the Idea's in God indeed are but one form: but in the Soul of the world they are many. They are placed in the minds of all other things, whether they be joyned to the body, or separated from the body, by a certain participation, and now by degrees are distinguished more, and more. They place them in nature, as certain small seed of forms infused by the Idea's, and lastly they place them in matter, as Shadows. Hereunto may be added, that in the Soul of the world there be as many Seminal Forms of things, as Idea's in the mind of God, by which forms she did in the Heavens above the Stars frame to her self shapes also, and stamped upon all these some properties; on these Stars therefore, shapes, and properties, all vertues of inferiour species, as also their properties do depend; so that every species hath its Celestiall shape, or figure that is sutable [suitable] to it from which also proceeds a wonderfull power of operating, which proper gift it receives from its own Idea, through the Seminal forms of the Soul of the world. For Idea's are not only essential causes of every species, but are also the causes of every vertue, which is in the species: and this is that which many Philosophers say, that the properties which are in the nature of things (which vertues indeed are the operations of the Idea's) are moved by certain vertues, viz. such as have a certain, and sure foundation, not fortuitous, nor casuall, but efficacious, powerfull, and sufficient, doing nothing in vain. Now these Vertues do not err in their actings, but by accident, viz. by reason of the impurity, or inequality of the matter: For upon this account there are found things of the same species, more, or less powerful, according to the purity, or indisposition of the matter; for all Celestial Influences may be hindred by the indisposition, and insufficiency of the matter. Whence it was a Proverb amongst the Platonists, That Celestial Vertues were infused according to the desert of the matter: Which also Virgil makes mention of, when he sings,

Their natures fiery are, and from above, And from gross bodies freed, divinely move.

Wherefore those things in which there is less of the Idea of the matter (i.e.) such things which have a greater resemblance of things separated, have more powerfull vertues in operation, being like to the operation of a separated Idea. We see then that the situation, and figure of Celestials is the cause of all those excellent Vertues, that are in inferiour species.

Chap. xii. How it is that particular Vertues are infused into particular Individuals, even of the same Species.
There are also in many Individuals, or particular things, peculiar gifts,

as wonderfull, as in the species, and these also are from the figure, and situation of Celestiall Stars. For every Individuall, when it begins to be under a determined Horoscope, and Celestiall Constellation, Contracts together with its essence a certain wonderfull vertue both of doing, and suffering something that is remarkable, even besides that which it receives from its species, and this it doth partly by the influence of the Heaven, and partly through that obedientialness of the matter of things to be generated, to the Soul of the World, which obedientialness indeed is such as that of our bodies to our souls. For we perceive that there is this in us, that according to our conceptions of things, our bodies are moved, and that cheerfully, as when we are afraid of, or fly from any thing. So many times when the Celestiall souls conceive several things, then the matter is moved obedientially to it: Also in Nature there appear divers prodigies, by reason of the imagination of superiour motions. So also they conceive, & imagine divers vertues, not only things naturall, but also sometimes things artificial, and this especially if the Soul of the operator be inclined towards the same. Whence Avicen saith, that whatsoever things are done here, must have been before in the motions, and conceptions of the Stars, and Orbes. So in things, various effects, inclinations, and dispositions are occasioned not only from the matter variously disposed, as many suppose, but from a various influence, and diverse form; not truly with a specifical difference, but peculiar, and proper. And the degrees of these are variously distributed by the first Cause of all things, God himself, who being unchangeable, distributes to every one as he pleaseth, with whom notwithstanding second Causes, Angelical and Celestial, cooperate, disposing of the Corporeal matter, and other things that are committed to them. All vertues therefore are infused by God, through the Soul of the World, yet by a particular power of resemblances, and intelligences over-ruling them, and concourse of the rayes, and aspects of the Stars in a certain peculiar harmonious consent.

Chap. xiii. Whence the Occult Vertues of things proceed.

It is well known to all, that there is a Certain vertue in the Loadstone, by which it attracts Iron, and that the Diamond doth by its presence take away that vertue of the Loadstone: so also Amber, and jeat [jet] rubbed, and warmed draw a straw to them, and the Stone Asbestus [asbestos] being once fired is never, or scarce extinguished: a Carbuncle shines in the dark, the Stone Aetites put above the young fruit of Women, or Plants, strengthens them, but being put under, causeth abortion; the Jasper stencheth [stauncheth] blood; the litle fish Echeneis stops the ships: Rhubarb expels choller [choler]; the liver of the Camelion [Chameleon] burnt, raiseth showers, and thunders. The Stone Heliotrope dazles [dazzles] the sight, and makes him that wears it to be invisible, the Stone Lyucurius takes away delusions from before the eyes, the perfume of the Stone Lypparis cals forth all the beasts, the Stone Synochitis brings up infernal Ghosts, the Stone Anachitis makes the images of the Gods appear. The Ennecis put under them that dream, causeth Oracles.

There is an Hearb [herb] in Æthiopia [Ethiopia], with which they report ponds, and lakes are dryed [dried] up, and all things that are shut, to be opened; and we read of an Hearb [herb] called Latace which the Persian Kings give to their Embassadours, that whithersoever they shall come, they shall abound with plenty of all things. There is also a Scythian Hearb [herb], with which being tasted, or at least held in the mouth, they report the Scythians will endure twelve dayes hunger, and thirst; and Apuleius saith, that he was taught by an Oracle that there were many kinds of Hearbs [herbs], and Stones, with which men might prolong their lives for ever, but that it was not lawfull for men to understand the knowledge of those things, because, whereas they have but a short time to live, they study mischief with all their might, and attempt all manner of wickedness; if they should be sure of a very long time, they would not spare the Gods themselves. But from whence these vertues are, none of all these have shewed, who have set forth huge Volumes of the properties of things, not Hermes, not Bochus, not Aaron, not Orpheus, not Theophrastus, not Thebith, not Zenothemis, not Zoroaster, not Evax, not Dioscorides, not Isaaick the Jew, not Zacharias the Babilonian [Babylonian], not Albertus, not Arnoldus; and yet all these have confessed the same, that Zacharias writes to Mithridites, that great power, and humane destinies are couched in the vertues of Stones and Hearbs [herbs]. But to know from whence these come, a higher speculation is required.

Alexander the peripateticke not going any further then his senses, and qualities, is of the opinion that these proceed from Elements, and their qualities, which haply might be supposed to be true, if those were of the same species; but many of the operations of the Stones agree neither in genere, nor specie. Therefore Plato, and his Schollers [scholars] attribute these vertues to Idea's, the formers of things. But Avicen reduceth these kinds of operations to Intelligencies, Hermes to the Stars, Albertus to the specificall forms of things. And although these Authors seem to thwart one the other, yet none of them, if they be rightly understood, goes beside the truth: since all their sayings are the same in effect in most things. For God in the first place is the end, and begining of all Vertues, he gives the seal of the Idea's to his servants the Intelligencies; who as faithfull officers sign all things intrusted [entrusted] to them with an Ideall Vertue, the Heavens, and Stars, as instruments, disposing the matter in the mean while for the receiving of those forms which reside in Divine Majesty (as saith Plato in Timeus) and to be conveyed by Stars; and the Giver of forms distributes them by the Ministry of his Intelligencies, which he hath set as Rulers, and Controllers over his Works, to whom such a power is intrusted in things committed to them, that so all Vertues of Stones, Hearbs [herbs], Metals, and all other things may come from the Intelligencies, the Governours. The Form therefore, and Vertue of things comes first from the Idea's, then from the ruling, and governing Intelligencies, then from the aspects of the Heavens disposing, and lastly from the tempers of the Elements disposed, answering the influencies of the Heavens, by which the Elements themselves are ordered, or disposed. These kinds of operations therefore are performed in these inferiour things by express forms, and in the Heavens by disposing vertues, in Intelligencies by mediating rules, in the original Cause by Idea's, and exemplary forms, all which must of necessity agree in the execution of the effect, and vertue of every thing.

There is therefore a wonderfull vertue, and operation in every Hearb [herb] and Stone, but greater in a Star, beyond which, even from the governing Intelligencies every thing receiveth, and obtains many things for it self, especially from the Supream Cause, with whom all things do mutually, and exactly correspond, agreeing in an harmonious consent, as it were in Hymnes, alwaies praising the highest Maker of all things, as by the three Children in the fiery furnace were all things called upon to praise God with singings.

Bless ye the Lord all things that grow upon the Earth, and all things which move in the Waters, all fowls of the Heavens, Beasts, and Cattle, together with the sons of men. There is therefore no other cause of the necessity of effects, then the connexion [connection] of all things with the first Cause, and their correspondency with those Divine patterns, and eternall Idea's, whence every thing hath its determinate, and particular place in the exemplary world, from whence it lives, and receives its originall being; And every vertue of Hearbs [herbs], Stones, Metals, Animals, Words, and Speeches, and all things that are of God, is placed there. Now the first Cause, which is God, although he doth by Intelligencies, and the Heavens work upon these inferiour things, doth sometimes (these Mediums being laid aside, or their officiating being suspended) works those things immediatly by himself, which works then are called Miracles: But whereas secondary causes, which Plato, and others call handmaids, do by the Command, and appointment of the first Cause, necessarily act, and are necessitated to produce their effects, if God shall notwithstanding according to his pleasure so discharge, and suspend them, that they shall wholly desist from the necessity of that Command, and appointment; then they are called the greatest Miracles of God. So the fire in the

Chaldeans furnace did not burn the Children: So also the Sun at the Command of Joshua went back from its course the space of one whole day; so also at the prayer of Hezekiah it went back ten degrees, or hours. So when Christ was Crucified the Sun was darkened, though at full Moon: And the reasons these operations can by no rationall discourse, no Magick, or occult, or profound Science whatsoever be found out, or understood, but are to be learned, and inquired into by Divine Oracles only.

Chap. xiv. Of the Spirit of the World, what it is, and how by way of medium it unites occult Vertues to their subjects.
Democritus and Orpheus, and many Pythagorians having most diligently searched into the vertues of Celestiall things, and natures of inferior things, said, That all things are full of God, and not without cause: For there is nothing of such transcending vertues, which being destitute of Divine assistance, is content with the nature of it self. Also they called those Divine Powers which are diffused in things, Gods: which Zoroaster called Divine allurements, Synesius Symbolicall inticements, others called them Lives, and some also Souls, saying, that the vertues of things did depend upon these; because it is the property of the Soul to be from one matter extended into divers things, about which it operates: So is a man, who extends his intellect unto intelligible things, and his imagination unto imaginable things; and this is that which they understood, when they said, viz. That the Soul of one thing went out, and went into another thing, altering it, and hindering the operations of it: As the Diamond hinders the operation of the Loadstone, that it cannot attract Iron. Now seeing the Soul is the first thing that is moveable, and as they say, is moved of it self; but the body, or the matter is of it self unable, and unfit for motion, and doth much degenerate from the Soul, therefore they say there is need of a more excellent Medium, viz. Such a one that may be as it were no body, but as it were a Soul, or as it were no Soul, but as it were a body, viz. by which the soul may be joyned to the

body.

Now they conceive such a medium to be the spirit of the World, viz. that which we call the quintessence: because it is not from the four Elements, but a certain first thing, having its being above, and besides them. There is therefore such a kind of spirit required to be, as it were the medium, whereby Celestiall Souls are joyned to gross bodies, and bestow upon them wonderfull gifts. This spirit is after the same manner in the body of the world, as ours is in the body of man. For as the powers of our soul are communicated to the members of the body by the spirit, so also the Vertue of the Soul of the World is diffused through all things by the quintessence: For there is nothing found in the whole world, that hath not a spark of the Vertue thereof. Yet it is more, nay most of all infused into those things which have received, or taken in most of this spirit: Now this spirit is received or taken in by the rayes of the Stars, so far forth as things render themselves conformable to them. By this spirit therefore every occult property is conveyed into Hearbs [herbs], Stones, Metals, and Animals, through the Sun, Moon, Planets, and through Stars higher then the Planets. Now this spirit may be more advantageous to us, if any one knew how to separate it from the Elements: or at least to use those things chiefly, which do most abound with this spirit. For these things, in which this spirit is less drowned in a body, and less checked by matter, do more powerfully, and perfectly act, and also more readily generate their like: for in it are all generative, & seminary Vertues. For which cause the Alchymists [alchemists] endeavour to separate this spirit from Gold, and Silver; which being rightly separated, and extracted, if thou shalt afterward project upon any matter of the same kind (i.e.) any Metall, presently will turn it into Gold, or Silver. And we know how to do that, and have seen it done: but we could make no more Gold, then the weight of that was, out of which we extracted the spirit. For seeing that is an extense form, and not intense, it cannot beyond its own bounds change and imperfect body into a perfect: which I deny not, but may be done by another way.

Chap. xv. How we must find out, and examine the Vertues of things by way of similitude.

It is now manifest that the occult properties in things are not from the nature of the Elements, but infused from above, hid from our senses, and scarce at last known by our reason, which indeed come from the Life, and the Spirit of the World, through the rayes of the Stars: and can no otherwise but by experience, and conjecture be enquired into by us. Wherefore, he that desires to enter upon this study must consider, that every thing moves, and turns it self to its like, and inclines that to it self with all its might, as well in property, viz. Occult vertue, as in quality, viz. Elementary vertue. Sometimes also in substance it self, as we see in Salt, for whatsoever hath long stood with Salt, becomes Salt: for every agent, when it hath begun to act, doth not attempt to make a thing inferiour to it self, but as much as may be, like, and sutable [suitable] to it self. Which also we

manifestly see in sensible Animals, in which the nutritive Vertue doth not change the meat into an Hearb [herb], or a Plant, but turns it into sensible flesh. In what things therefore there is an excess of any quality, or property, as heat, cold, boldness, fear, sadness, anger, love, hatred, or any other passion, or Vertue; whether it be in them by nature, or sometimes also by art, or chance, as boldness in a harlot; these things do very much move, and provoke to such a quality, passion, or Vertue. So Fire moves to Fire, and Water moves to Water, and be that is bold moves to boldness. And it is well known amongst Physitians [physicians], that brain helps the brain, and lungs, the lungs. So also it is said, that the right eye of a Frog helps the soreness of a mans right eye, and the left eye thereof helps the soreness of his left eye, if they be hanged about his neck in a Cloth of its naturall Colour: The like is reported of the eyes of a Crab. So the foot of a Tortoise helps them that have the Gout in their being applyed thus, as foot to foot, hand to hand, right to right, left to left.

After this manner they say, that any Animall that is barren causeth another to be barren; and of the Animall, especially the Testicles, Matrix [womb], or Urin [urine]. So they report that a woman shall not conceive, if she drink every moneth of the Urin [urine] of a Mule, or any thing steeped in it. If therefore we would obtain any property or Vertue, let us seek for such Animals, or such other things whatsoever, in which such a property is in a more eminent manner then in any other thing, and in these let us take that part in which such a property, or Vertue is most vigorous: as if at any time we would promote love, let us seek some Animall which is most loving, of which kind are Pigeons, Turtles, Sparrows, Swallows, Wagtailes: and in these take those members, or parts, in which the Venerall [venereal, i.e. sexual] appetite is most vigorous, such as the heart, testicles, matrix [womb], yard [penis], sperme, and menstrues. And it must be done at that time when these Animals have this affection most intense: for then they do provoke, and draw love. In like manner to increase boldness, let us look for a Lyon [lion], or a Cock, and of these let us take the heart, eyes, or forehead. And so we must understand that which Psellus the Platonist saith, viz. that Dogs, Crows, and Cocks conduce much to watchfulness: also the Nightingale, and Bat, and horn Owle [horned owl], and in these the heart, head, and eyes especially. Therefore it is said, if any shall carry the heart of a Crow, or a Bat about him, he shall not sleep till he cast it away from him. The same doth the head of a Bat dryed [dried], and bound to the right arme of him that is awake, for if it be put upon him when he is asleep, it is said, that he shall not be awaked till it be taken off from him. After the same manner doth a Frog, and an Owle make one talkative and of these specially the tongue, and heart; So the tongue also of a Water-frog laid under the head, makes a man speak in his sleep, and the heart of a scrich-Owle [screech-owl] laid upon the left breast of a woman that is asleep is said to make her utter all her secrets. The same also the heart of the horn Owle [horned owl] is said to do, also the sewet [suet] of a Hare laid upon the breast of one that is asleep. Upon the same account do Animals that are long lived, conduce to long life; and whatsoever things have a power in themselves, to renew themselves, conduce to the renovation of our body, and restoring of youth, which Physitians [physicians] have often professed they know to be true; as is manifest of the Viper, and Snake. And it is known that Harts renew their old age by the eating of Snakes. After the same manner the Phoenix is renewed by a fire which she makes for her self; and the like vertue there is in a Pellican [pelican], whose right foot being put under warm dung, after three moneths [months] there is of that generated a Pellican [pelican]. Therefore some Physitians [physicians] by some certain confections made of Vipers, and Hellebor [hellebore], and the flesh of some such kind of Animals do restore youth, and indeed do sometimes restore it so, as Medea restored old Pileas. It is also believed that the blood of a Bear, if it be sucked out of her wound, doth increase strength of body, because that Animall is the strongest creature.

Chap. xvi. How the operations of several Vertues pass from one thing into another, and are communicated one to the other.

Thou must know, that so great is the power of naturall things, that they not only work upon all things that are neer them, by their Vertue, but also besides this, they infuse into them a like power, through which by the same Vertue they also work upon other things, as we see in the Loadstone, which Stone indeed doth not only draw Iron Rings, but also infuseth a Vertue into the Rings themselves, whereby they can do the same, which Austin [Augustine] and Albertus [Magnus] say they saw. After this manner it is, as they say, that a common harlot, grounded in boldness, and impudence doth infect all that are neer her, by this property, whereby they are made like her self. Therefore they say that if any one shall put on the inward garment of an Harlot, or shall have about him that looking glass, which she daily looks into, he shall thereby become bold, confident, impudent, and wanton. In like manner they say, that a cloth that was about a dead Corpse hath received from thence the property of sadness, and melancholy;

and that the halter wherewith a man was hanged hath certain wonderfull properties. The like story tels Pliny, if any shall put a green Lizard made blind, together with Iron, or Gold Rings into a glass-vessel, putting under them some earth, and then shutting the vessel, and when it appears that the Lizard hath received his sight, shall put him out of the glass, that those Rings shall help sore eyes. The same may be done with Rings, and a Weesel [weasel], whose eyes after they are with any kind of prick put out, it is certain are restored to sight again. Upon the same account Rings are put for a certain time in the nest of Sparrows, or Swallows, which afterwards are used to procure love, and favor.

Chap. xvii. How by enmity and friendship the vertues of things are to be tryed, and found out.

In the next place it is requisite that we consider that all things have a friendliness, and enmity amongst themselves, and every thing hath something that it fears & dreads, that is an enemy, and destructive to it; and on the contrary something that it rejoyceth, and delighteth in, and is strengthened by. So in the Elements, Fire is an enemy to Water, and Aire to Earth, but yet they agree amongst themselves. And again, in Celestiall bodies, Mercury, Jupiter, the Sun, and Moon are friends to Saturn; Mars, and Venus enemies to him, all the Planets besides Mars are friends to Jupiter, also all besides Venus hate Mars; Jupiter, and Venus love the Sun, Mars, Mercury, and the Moon are enemies to him, all besides Saturne love Venus; Jupiter, Venus, and Saturne are friends to Mercury, the Sun, Moon, and Mars his enemies. Jupiter, Venus, Saturne are friends to the Moon, Mars, and Mercury her enemies. There is another kind of enmity amongst the Stars, viz. when they have opposite houses; as Saturne to the Sun and Moon, Jupiter to Mercury, Mars to Venus. And their enmity is stronger, whose exaltations are opposite: as of Saturne, and the Sun; of Jupiter, and Mars; of Venus, and Mercury. But their friendship is the strongest, who agree in nature, quality, substance, and power; as Mars with the Sun, as Venus with the Moon, as Jupiter with Venus, as also their friendship whose exaltation is in the house of another, as that of Saturne with Venus, of Jupiter with the Moon, of Mars with Saturn, of the Sun with Mars, of Venus with Jupiter, of the Moon with Venus. And of what sort the friendships, and enmities of the superiours be, such are the inclinations of things subjected to them in these inferiour. These dispositions therefore of friendship, and enmity are nothing else but certain inclinations of things of the one to another, desiring such, and such a thing if it be absent, and to move towards it, unless it be hindered, and to acquiess [acquiesce] in it when it is obtained, shunning the contrary, and dreading the approach of it, and not resting in, or being contented with it. Heraclitus therefore being guided by this opinion, professed that all things were made by enmity & friendship. Now the inclinations of Friendship are such in Vegetables and Minerals, as is that attractive inclination, which the Loadstone hath upon Iron, and the Emrald [emerald] upon riches, and favour; the Jasper upon the birth of any thing, and the Stone Achates upon Eloquence; In like manner there is a kind of Bituminous Clay that draws Fire, and leaps into it, wheresoever it sees it: Even so doth the root of the Hearb [herb] Aproxis draw Fire from afar off. Also the same inclination there is betwixt the male palme, and female: whereof when the bough of one shall touch the bough of the other, they fold themselves into mutual embraces, neither doth the female bring forth fruit without the male. And the Almond tree, when she is alone is less fruitfull. The Vines love the Elme, and the Olive- tree, and myrtle love one the other: also the Olive-tree, and Fig tree. Now in Animals there is amity betwixt the Blackbird, and Thrush, betwixt the Crow, and Heron, betwixt Peacocks, and Pigeons, Turtles, and Parrats [parrots]. Whence Sappho writes to Phaon.

To Birds unlike oftimes joyned are white Doves; Also the Bird that's green, black Turtle loves.

Again, the Whale, and the little Fish his guide are friendly. Neither is this amity in Animals amongst themselves, but also with other things, as with Metals, Stones, and Vegetables, so the Cat delights in the Hearb [herb] Nip [catnip], by rubbing her self upon which she is said to conceive without a male; and there be Mares in Cappadocia, that expose themselves to the blast of the wind, and by the attraction thereof conceive. So Frogs, Toads, Snakes, and all manner of creeping poisonous things delight in the Plant called Pas-flower, of whom, as the Physitians [physicians] say, if any one eat, he shall dye [die] with laughing. The Tortoise also when he is hunted by the Adder, eats Origanum [origano], and is thereby strengthened: and the Stork, when he hath eat Snakes, seeks for a remedy in Origanum [origano]: and the Weesell [weasel], when he goes to fight with the Basilisk, eats Rue, whence we come to know that Origanum [origano], and Rue are effectuall against poison. So in some Animals there is an imbred skil, and medicinall art; for when the Toad is wounded with a bite or poison of another Animall, he is wont to go to Rue, or Sage, and Rub the place wounded, and so escapes the danger of the poison. So men have learned many excellent remedies of diseases, & vertues of things from bruits [brutes]; So Swallows have shewed us that Sallendine is very medicinable for the sight, with which they cure the eyes of their young, and the pye when she is sick, puts a Bay-leafe into her nest, and is recovered. In like maner, Cranes, Dawes [jackdaws], Partriges [partridges], Blackbirds purge their nauseous stomacks [stomachs] with the same, with which also Crows allay the poison of the Chameleon; and the Lyon [lion], if he be feavorish [feverish], is recovered by eating of an Ape. The Lapwing being surfetted [surfeited] with eating of Grapes, cures himself with Southernwood; so the Harts have taught us that the Hearb [herb] Ditany is very good to draw out Darts; for they being wounded with an Arrow, cast it out by eating of this Hearb [herb]: the same do Goats in Candy. So Hinds, a little before they bring forth, purge themselves with a certain Hearb [herb] called Mountain Osier. Also they that are hurt with Spiders, seek a remedy by eating of Crabs: Swine also being hurt by Snakes cure themselves by eating of them; and Crows when they perceive they are poisoned with a kinde of French poison, seek for cure in the

Oake; Elephants, when they have swallowed a Chameleon help themselves with the wild olive. Bears being hurt with Mandrakes, escape the danger by eating of Pismires [ants]. Geese, Ducks, and such like watery fowle, cure themselves with the Hearb [herb] called will-sage. Pigeons, Turtles, Hens, with the Hearb [herb] called Pellitory of the wall. Cranes with Bull-rushes [bulrushes]. Leopards cure themselves, being hurt, with the HEarb [herb] called Wolfes-bane, by mans dung: Boars with Ivy, Hinds with the Hearb [herb] called Cinnara.

Chapter xviii. Of the Inclinations of Enmities.

On the contrary there are inclinations of Emnities, and they are as it were the odium, and anger, indignation, and a certain kind of obstinate contrariety of nature, so that any thing shuns its contrary, and drives it away out of its presence. Such kinds of inclinations hath Rhubarb against Choller [choler], Treacle against poison, the Saphir [sapphire] Stone against hot biles [boils], and feavorish [feverish] heats, and diseases of the eyes; the Amethyst against drunkenness, the Jasper against Flux of blood, and offensive imaginations, the Emrald [emerald], and Agnus Castus against Lust, Achates against poison, Piony [peony] against the Falling sickness, Corall against the ebullition of black Choller [choler], and pains of the stomack [stomach]. The Topaze against spirituall heats, such as are covetousness, lust, and all manner of excesses of love. The like inclination is there also of Pismire [ants] against the Hearb [herb] Origanum [origano], and the wing of a Bat, and the heart of a Lapwing, from the presence of which they flie [fly]. Also Origanum [origano] is contrary to a certain poisonous fly, which cannot endure the Sun, and resists Salamanders, and loathes Cabbage with such a deadly hatred, that they destroy one the other; so Cucumbers hate oile, and will run themselves into a ring least they should touch it. And it is said that the Gall of a Crow makes men afraid, and drives them sway from where it is, as also certain other things; so a Diamond doth disagree with the Loadstone, that being set by it, it will not suffer Iron to be drawn to it; and sheep flie [fly] from Frog-parsley as from some deadly thing: and that which is more wonderfull, nature hath pictured the sign of this death in the livers of sheep, in which the very figure of Frog- parsley being described, doth naturally appear; So Goats do so hate garden basil, as if there were nothing more pernicious. And again, amongst Animals, Mice, and Weesels [weasels] do disagree; whence it is said that Mice will not touch Cheese, if the brains of a Weesel [weasel] be put in the rennet, and besides that the Cheese will not be corrupt with age. So a Lizard is so contrary to Scorpions, that it makes them afraid with its very sight, as also it puts them into a cold sweat; therefore they are killed with the oile of them, which oile also cures the wounds made by Scorpions. There is also an enmity betwixt Scorpions, and Mice: wherefore if a Mouse be applyed to a prick or wound made by a Scorpion, it cures it, as it is reported. There is also an enmity betwixt Scorpions, and Stalabors, Aspes, and Waspes. It is reported also that nothing is so much an enemy to Snakes as Crabs, and that if Swine be hurt therewith they eat them, and are cured. The Sun also being in Cancer, Serpents are tormented. Also the Scorpion, and Crocodile kil [kill] one the other; and if the Bird Ibis doth but touch a crocodile with one of his feathers, he makes him immovable; the Bird called Bustard flies away at the sight of a horse; and a Hart runs away at the sight of a Ram, as also of a Viper. An Elephant trembles at the hearing of the grunting of a Hog, so doth a Lyon [lion] at the sight of a Cock: And Panthers will not touch them that are annointed [anointed] all over with the broth of a Hen, especially if Garlick hath been boiled in it. There is also enmity betwixt Foxes, and Swans, Buls [bulls], and Daws [jackdaws]. Amongst Birds also some are at a perpetuall strife one with another, as also with other Animals, as Daws [jackdaws], and Owles, the Kite, and Crows, the Turtle, and Ring-taile, Egepis, and Eagles, Harts, and Dragons. Also amongst Water Animals there is enmity, as betwixt Dolphins, and Whirpools, Mullets, and Pikes, Lampreys, and Congers: Also the fish called Pourcontrel makes the Lobster so much afraid, that the Lobster seeing the other but neer him, is struck dead. The Lobster, and Conger tear one the other. The Civet Cat is said to stand so in awe of the Panther, that he hath no power to resist him, or touch his skin: and they say that if the skins of both of them be hanged up one against the other, the haires of the Panthers skin fall off. And Orus Apollo saith in his Hieroglyphicks, if any one be girt about with the skin of the Civet Cat, that he may pass safely through the middle of his enemies, and not at all be afraid. Also the Lamb is very much afraid of the Wolf, and flies from him. And they say that if the taile, or skin, or head of a Wolf be hanged upon the sheep-coate, the sheep are much troubled, and cannot eat their meat for fear. And Pliny makes mention of a Bird, called Marlin, that breaks Crows Eggs; whose young are so annoyed by the Fox that she also will pinch, and pull the Foxes whelps, and the Fox her self also: which when the Crows see, they help the Fox against her, as against a common enemy. The litle Bird called a Linnet living in Thistles, hates Asses, because they eat the Flowers of Thistles. Also there is such a bitter enmity betwixt the litle bird called Esalon, and the Asse, that their blood will not mix together, and that at the braying of the Asse both the eggs and young of the Esalon perish. There is also such a dis-agreement betwixt the Olive-tree and a Harlot, that if she Plant it, it will either be always unfruitfull, or altogether wither. A Lyon [lion] fears nothing so much as fired Torches, and will be tamed by nothing so much as by these: and the Wolf fears neither sword, nor spear, but a stone, by the throwing of which a wound being made, worms breed in the Wolf. A Horse fears a Camell, so that he cannot endure to see so much as his picture. An Elephant when he rageth, is quieted by see-ing of a Cock. A Snake is afraid of a man that is naked, but pursues a man that is clothed. A mad Bull is tamed by being tyed to a Fig-tree. Amber draws all things to it besides Garden Basill, and those things, which are smeared with oile, betwixt which there is a kinde of a nat-urall Antipathy.

Chapter xix. How the Vertues of things are to be tryed and found out, which are in them specifically, or in any one Individuall by way of speciall gift.

Moreover thou must consider that the Vertues of things are in some things according to the species, as boldness, and courage in a Lyon [lion], & Cock: fearfulness in a Hare, or Lamb, ravenousness in a Wolf, treachery, and deceitfulness in a Fox, flattery in a Dog, covetousness in a Crow, and Daw [jackdaw], pride in a Horse, anger in a Tygre [tiger], and Boar, sadness, and melancholy in a Cat, lust in a sparrow, and so of the rest. For the greatest part of naturall Vertues doth follow the species. Yet some are in things individually; as there be some men which do so wonderfully abhor the sight of a Cat, that they cannot look upon her without quaking; which fear it is manifest is not in them as they are men. And Avicen tels of a man that lived in his time, whom all poisonous things did shun, all of them dying, which did by chance bite him, he himself not being hurt, and Albertus reports that in a City of the Ubians he saw a wench who would catch Spiders to eat them, and being much pleased with such a kind of meat, was wonderfully nourished therewith. So is boldness in a Harlot, fearfulness in a Thief. And upon this account it is that Philosophers say, that any particular thing that never was sick, is good against any manner of sickness: therefore they say that a bone of a dead man, who never had a feavor [fever], being laid upon the patient, frees him of his quartane. There are also many singular vertues infused into particular things by Celestiall bodies, as we have shewed before.

Chapter xx. That naturall Vertues are in some things throughout their whole substance, and in other things in certain parts, and members.

Again thou must consider, that the vertues of things are in some things in the whole (i.e.) the whole substance of them, or in all their parts, as that little fish Echeneis, which is said to stop a ship by its meer touch, this it doth not do according to any particular part, but according to the whole substance. So the Civet Cat hath this in its whole substance, that Dogs by the very touch of his shadow hold their peace. So Salendine is good for the sight, not according to any one but all its parts, not more in the root then in the leaves, and seeds; and so of the rest. But some vertues are in things according to some parts of it, viz. only in the tongue, or eyes, or some other members, and parts; so in the eyes of a Basilisk, is a most violent power to kill men, assoon as they see them: the like power is there in the eyes of the Civet Cat, which makes any Animall that it hath looked upon, to stand still, to be amazed, and not able to move it self. The like vertue is there in the eyes of some Wolfes [wolves], which if they see a man first, make him amazed, and so hoarse, that if he would cry out, he hath not the use of his voice: Of this Virgil makes mention, when he sings,

Moeris is dumb, hath lost his voice, and why? The Wolf on Moeris first hath cast his eye.

So also there were some certain women in Scythia, and amongst the Illyrians, and
Triballians, who as often as they looked angrily upon any man, were said to slay him.

Also we read of a certain people of Rhodes, called Telchines, who corrupted all things with their sight, wherefore Jupiter drowned them. Therefore Witches, when they would after this manner work by witchcraft, use the eyes of such kind of Animals in their waters for the eyes, for the like effects. In like manner do Pismires [ants] fly from the heart of a Lapwing, not from the head, foot, or eyes. So the gall of Lizards being bruised in Water is said to gather Weesels [weasels] together, not the taile or the head of it; and the gall of Goats put into the Earth in a brazen Vesel [vessel], gathers Frogs together; and a Goats liver is an enemy to Butterflies and all Maggots, and dogs shun them that have the heart of a Dog about them, and Foxes will not touch those poultry that have eaten the liver of a Fox. So divers things have divers vertues dispersed variously through several parts, as they are from above infused into them according to the diversity of things to be received; as in a mans body the bones receive nothing but life, the eyes sight, the ears hearing. And there is in mans body a certain little bone, which the Hebrews call LVZ, of the bigness of a pulse that is husked, which is subject to no corruption, neither is it overcome with Fire, but is alwaies preserved unhurt, out of which, as they say, as a Plant out of the seed, our Animall bodies shall in the Resurrection of the dead spring up. And these vertues are not cleared by reason, but by experience.

3

Section 3

Chapter xxi. Of the Vertues of things which are in them only in their life time, and such as remain in them even after their death. Moreover we must know that there are some properties in things only whilest they live, and some that remain after their death. So the litle fish Echeneis stops the ships, and the Basilisk, and Catablepa kill with their sight, when they are alive; but when they are dead do no such thing. So they say that in the Colick, if a live Duck be applyed to the belly, it takes away the pain, and her self dies: like to this is that which Archytas sayes. If you take a heart newly taken out of an Animall, and whilest it is yet warm, and hang it upon one that hath a quartane feavor [fever], it drives it away. So if any one swallow the heart of a Lapwing, or a Swallow, or a Weesel [weasel], or a Mole whilest it is yet warm with naturall heat, it shall be helpfull to him for remembring [remembering], understanding, and foretelling: Hence is this generall rule, viz. That whatsoever things are taken out of Animals, whether they be Stones, any Member, Excrements, as Haire, Dung, Nailes, they must be taken from those Animals, whilest they be yet living; and if it be possible, that so they may be alive afterwards. Whence they say, when you take the tongue of a Frog, you must put the Frog into the water again; and if you take the tooth of a Wolf, you must not kill the Wolf; and so of the rest. So writes Democritus, if any one take out the tongue of a water-Frog, yet living, no other part of the body sticking to it, and she be let go into the Water again, & lay it upon the place where the heart beats, of a woman, she shall answer truly whatsoever you ask her. Also they say, that if the eyes of a Frog be before Sun rising bound to the sick party, and the Frog be let go again blind into the Water, they will drive away tertian ague; as also that they will, being bound with the flesh of a Nightingale in the skin of a Hart, keep one alwaies watchfull without sleep. Also the ray of the fork fish being bound to the Navil [navel], is said to make a woman have an easie travel, if it be taken from it alive, and it put into the Sea again. So they say the right eye of a Serpent being applyed, doth help the watering of the eyes, if the Serpent be let go alive. And there is a certain fish, or great Serpent called Myrus, whose eye, if it be pulled out, and bound to the forehead of the patient, is said to cure the inflamation [inflammation] of the eyes, and that the eye of the fish grows again, and that he is taken blind that did not let the fish go. Also the teeth of all Serpents, being taken out whilest they are alive, and hanged about the patient, are said to cure the quartane. So doth the tooth of a Mole taken out whilest she is alive, being afterwards let go, cure the tooth-ach [toothache]; and Dogs will not bark at those that have the taile of a Weesel [weasel] that is escaped. And Democritus relates that the tongue of a Chameleon, if it be taken from her alive, doth conduce to a good success in trials, and is profitable for women that are in travel, if it be about the outside of the house, for you must take heed that it be not brought into the house, because that would be most dangerous; Moreover there be some properties that remain after death: and of these the Platonists say, that they are things in which the Idea of the matter is less swallowed up, in these, even after death that which is immortall in them, doth not cease to work wonderfull things. So in the Hearbs [herbs], and Plants pulled asunder, and dryed, that vertue is quick, and operative which was infused at first into them by the Idea. Thence it is, that as the Eagle all her life time doth overcome all other birds: so also her feathers after her death destroy, and consume the feathers of all other birds. Upon the same account doth a Lyons [lion's] skin destroy all other skins: and the skin of the Civet Cat destroyes the skin of the Panther: and the skin of a Wolf corrodes the skin of a Lamb: And some of these do not do it by way of a corporeall contact, but also sometimes by their very sound. So a drum made of the skin of a Wolf, makes a drum made of a Lamb skin not to sound. Also a drum made of the skin of the fish called Rotchet, drives away all creeping things, at what distance so-ever the sound of it is heard: and the strings of an instrument made of the guts [intestines] of a Wolf, and being strained [strung] upon a Harp, or Lute with strings made of sheeps guts, will make no harmony.

Chapter xxii. How inferior things are subjected to superior bodies, and how the bodies, the actions, and dispositions of men are ascribed to Stars, and Signes.

It is manifest that all things inferiour are subject to the superiour, and after a manner (as saith Proclus) they are one in the other, viz. in inferiour are superiour, and in superiour are inferiour: so in the Heaven are things Terrestriall, but as in their cause, and in a Celestiall manner; and in the Earth are things Celestiall, but after a Terrestriall manner, as in an effect. So we say that there be here certain things which are Solary, and certain which are Lunary, in which the Sun, and Moon make a strong impression of their vertue. Whence it is that these kind of things receive more operations, and properties, like to those of the Stars, & Signes which they are under: So we know that Solary things respect the heart, & head, by reason that Leo is the house of the Sun, and Aries the exaltation of the Sun: so things under Mars are good for the head, and testicles, by reason of Aries, and Scorpio. Hence they whose senses faile, and heads ake [ache] by reason of drunkenness, if they put their testicles into cold Water, or wash them with Vinegar, find present help.

But in reference to these it is necessary to know how mans body is distributed to Planets, & Signes. Know therefore that according to the doctrine of the Arabians, the Sun rules over the brain, heart, the thigh, the marrow, the right eye, and the spirit; also the tongue, the mouth, and the rest of the Organs of the senses, as well internall as externall; also the hands, feet, legs, nerves, and the power of imagination. That Mercury rules over the spleen, stomack [stomach], bladder, womb, and right ear, as also the faculty of the common sense. That Saturn rules over the liver and fleshy part of the stomack [stomach]. That Jupiter over the belly, and navill [navel], whence it is written by the Ancients, that the effigies of a navil [navel] was laid up in the temple of Jupiter Hammon. Also some attribute to him the ribs, breast, bowels, blood, arms, and the right hand, and left ear, and the powers natural. And some set Mars over the blood, and veins, the kidnies [kidneys], the bag of the gall [gall bladder], the buttocks, the back, motion of the sperm, and the irascible power. Again they set Venus over the kidnies [kidneys], the testicles, the privities, the womb, the seed, and concupiscible power; as also the flesh, fat, belly, breast, navill [navel], and all such parts as server to venerall [venereal] acts, also the Os sacrum, the back bone [backbone], and loins; as also the head, mouth, with which they give a kiss, as a token of love. Now the Moon, although she may challenge the whole body, and every member thereof according to the variety of the Signes: yet more particularly they ascribe to her the brain, lungs, marrow of the back bone [backbone], the stomack [stomach], the menstrues, and all other excrements, and the left eye, as also the power of increasing. But Hermes saith, That there are seven holes in the head of an Animall, distributed to the seven Planets, viz. the right ear to Saturne, the left to Jupiter, the right nostrell [nostril] to Mars, the left to Venus, the right eye to the Sun, the left to the Moon, and the mouth to Mercury. The severall Signes also of the Zodiack take care of their members. So Aries governs the head, and face, Taurus the neck, Gemini the armes, and shoulders, Cancer the breast, lungs, stomack [stomach], and armes, Leo heart, stomack [stomach], liver, and back, Virgo the bowels, and bottome of the stomack [stomach], Libra the kidnies [kidneys], thighs, and buttocks, Scorpius [Scorpio] the genitals, the privities, and womb, Sagittarius the thigh, and groins, Capricornus the knees, Aquarius the legs and shins, Pisces the feet. And as the triplicities of these Signes answer one the other, and agree in Celestials, so also they agree in the members, which is sufficiently manifest by experience, because with the coldness of the feet, the belly, and breast are affected, which members answer the same triplicity; whence it is, if a medicine be applyed to the one, it helps the other, as by the warming of the feet, the pain of the belly ceaseth. Remember therefore this order, and know, that things which are under any one of the Planets, have a certain particular aspect, or inclination to those members that are attributed to that Planet, and especially to the houses, and exaltations thereof. For the rest of the dignities, as those triplicities, and markes, and face, are of litle account in this; upon this account therefore Piony [peony], Balme, Clove-gilliflowers, Citron-pils, sweet Marjoram, Cynnamon [cinnamon], Saffron, Lignum Aloes, Frankincense, Amber, Musk, and Myrrh help the head, and heart; by reason of sol [the Sun], Aries, and Leo: so doth Rib-wort, the Hearb [herb] of Mars, help the head, and testicles by reason of Aries, and Scorpio: and so of the rest. Also all things under Saturne conduce to sadness, and melancholly [melancholy]; those under Jupiter to mirth, and honour; those under Mars to boldness, contention, and anger; those under the Sun to glory, victory and courage; those under Venus to love, lust, and concupiscence; those under Mercury to Eloquence; those under the Moon to a common life. Also all the actions, and dispositions of men are distributed according to the Planets. For Saturne governes old men, Monkes, melancholly [melancholy] men, and hid treasures; and those things which are obtained with long journies [journeys], and difficulty; but Jupiter, those that are Religious, Prelates, Kings, and Dukes, and such kind of gains that are got lawfully: Mars rules over Barbers, Chirurgeons, Physitians [physicians], Sergeants, Executioners, Butchers, all that make fires, Bakers, Souldiers [soldiers], who are every where called Martial men.

Also do the other Stars signifie their office, as they are described in the books of Astrologers.

Chapter xxiii. How we shall know what Stars naturall things are under, and what things are under the Sun, which are called Solary.
Now it is very hard to know, what Star, or Signe every thing is under: yet it is known through the imitation of their rayes, or motion, or figure of the superiours. Also some of them are known by their colours and odours, also some by the effects of their operations, answering to some Stars. So then Solary things, or things under the power of the Sun are, amongst Elements, the lucid flame; in the humours, the purer blood, and spirlt of life; amongst tasts [tastes], that which is quick, mixed with sweetness. Amongst Metals, Gold by reason of its splendor, and its receiving that from the Sun which makes it cordiall. And amongst stones, they which resemble the rayes of the Sun by their golden sparklings, as doth the glittering stone Aetites which hath power against the Falling-sickness, and poisons: so also the stone, which is called the eye of the Sun, being of a figure like to the Apple of the eye, from the middle whereof shines forth a ray, it comforts the brain, and strengthens the sight; So the Carbuncle which shines by night, hath a vertue against all aiery, and vaporous poison: so the Chrysolite stone is of a light green colour, in which, when it is held against the Sun, there shines forth a golden Star; and this comforts those parts that serve for breathing, & helps those that be Asthmaticall, and if it be bored through, and the hole filled with the Mane of an Asse, and bound to the left arme, it drives away idle imaginations, and melancholy fears, and puts away foolishness: So the stone called Iris, which is like Crystall in colour, being often found with six corners, when under some roof part of it is held against the rayes of the Sun, and the other part is held in the shadow, it gathers the rayes of the Sun into it self, which, whilest it sends them forth, by way of reflection, makes a Rain-bow [rainbow] appear on the opposite wall. Also the Stone Heliotropion [heliotrope] green like the Jasper, or Emrald

[emerald], beset with red specks [i.e. bloodstone], makes a man constant, renowned, and famous, also it conduceth to long life: And the vertue of it indeed is most wonderfull upon the beams of the Sun, which it is said to turn into blood (i.e.) to appear of the colour of blood, as if the Sun were eclypsed [eclipsed], viz. When it is joyned to the juice of a Hearb [herb] of the same name, and be put into a vessell of Water: There is also another vertue of it more wonderfull, and that is upon the eyes of men, whose sight it doth so dim, and dazel [dazzle], that it doth not suffer him that carries it to see it, & this it doth not do without the help of the Hearb [herb] of the same name, which also is called Heliotropium [heliotrope], (i.e.) following the Sun. These vertues doth Albertus Magnus, and William of Paris confirm in their writings. The Hyacinth also hath a vertue from the Sun against poisons, and pestiferous vapours; it makes him that carries it to be safe, and acceptable; it conduceth also to riches, and wit, it strengthens the heart; being held in the mouth, it doth wonderfully cheer up the mind. Also there is the stone Pyrophylus, of a red mixture, which Albertus Magnus saith Æsculapius, makes mention of in one of his Epistles unto Octavius Augustus, saying, that there is a certain poison so wonderfull cold, which preserves the heart of man being taken out from burning, so that if for any time it be put into the Fire, it is turned into a stone, and this is that stone which is called Pyrophylus, from the fire. It hath a wonderfull vertue against poison, and it makes him that carries it, to be renowned and dreadfull to his enemies. But above all, that stone is most Solary, which Apollonius is reported to have found, and which is called Pantaura, which draws other stones to it, as the Loadstone doth Iron, most powerfull against all poisons; it is called by some Pantherus, because it is spotted like the beast called the Panther. It is therefore also called Pantochras, because it contains all colours. Aaron cals it Evanthum. There are also other Solary stones, as the Topazius, Chrysopassus, the Rubine, and Balagius. So also is Auripigmentum, and things of a golden colour, and very lucid.

Amongst plants also and trees, those are Solary, which turn towards the Sun, as the Marygold [marigold], and those which fold in their leaves when the Sun is neer upon setting, but when it riseth unfold their leaves by little and little. The Lote-tree also is Solary, as is manifest by the figure of the fruit & leaves. So also Piony [peony], Sallendine, Balme, Ginger, Gentian, Dittany, & Vervin [vervain], which is of use in prophecying [prophesying], and expiations, as also driving away evill spirits. The Bay- tree also is consecrated to Phoebus, so is the Cedar, the Palm tree, the ash, the Ivie [ivy], and Vine, and whatsoever repell poisons, and lightnings, and those things which never fear the extremities of the Winter. Solary also are Mint, Mastick, Zedoary, Saffron, Balsome [balsam], Amber, Musk, Yellow honey, Lignum aloes, Cloves, Cinnamon, Calamus, Aromaticus, Pepper, Frankincense, sweet Marjoram, also Libanotis, which Orpheus cals the sweet perfume of the Sun. Amongst Animals those are Solary which are magnanimous, couragious [courageous], ambitious of victory, and renown: as the Lyon [lion], King of beasts, the Crocodile, the spotted Wolf, the Ram, the Boar, the Bull, King of the herd, which was by the Egyptians at Heliopolis dedicated to the Sun, which they called Verites; and an Ox was consecrated to Apis in Memphi [Memphis], and in Herminthus a Bull by the name of Pathis. The Wolf also was consecrated to Apollo, and Latona. Also the beast called Baboon is Solary, which twelve times in a day, viz. every hour barks, and in time of Equinoctium [equinox] pisseth [urinates] twelve times every hour: the same also it doth in the night, whence the Egyptians did Engrave him upon their Fountains. Also amongst birds these are Solary, The Phoenix, being but one of that kind, and the Eagle, the Queen of birds, also the Vulture, the Swan, and those which sing at the rising Sun, and as it were call upon it to rise, as the Cock, Crow, also the Hawk, which because it in the Divinity of the Egyptians is an emblem of the spirit, and light, is by Porphyrius [Porphyry] reckoned amongst the Solary birds. Moreover, all such things as have some resemblance of the works of the Sun, as Worms shining in the night, and the Betle [beetle], which is a creature that lies under Cow-dung, also according to Appious interpretation, such whose eyes are changed according to the course of the Sun, are accounted Solary, and those things which come of them. And amongst fish, the Sea Calf is chiefly Solary, who doth resist lightning, also shell fish, and the fish called Pulmo, both which shine in the night, and the fish called Stella [i.e. starfish] for his parching heat, and the fish called Strombi [i.e. strombite or sea-snail], that follow their King, and Margari [i.e. oyster], which also have a King, and being dryed, are hardened into a stone of a golden colour.

Chapter xxiv. What things are Lunary, or under the power of the Moon.

These things are Lunary, amongst the Elements, viz. the Earth, then the Water, as well that of the Sea, as of the Rivers, and all moist things, as the moisture of Trees, and Animals, especially they which are White, as the Whites of Eggs, fat, sweat, flegme [phlegm], and the superfluities of bodies. Amongst tasts [tastes], salt, and insipid; amongst Metals, Silver; amongst stones, Crystall, the Silver Marcasite, and all those stones that are White, and Green. Also the stone Selenites (i.e.) Lunary, shining from a white body, with a yellow brightness, imitating the motion of the Moon, having in it the figure of the Moon which daily increaseth, or decreaseth as doth the Moon. Also Pearls, which are generated in shels [shells] of fishes from the droppings of Water, also the Berill [beryl]. Amongst Plants and Trees, these are Lunary, as the Selenotropion, which turns towards the Moon, as doth the Heliotropion towards the Sun, and the Palme tree sends forth a bough at every rising of the Moon; Hyssope also, and Rosemary, Agnus Castu, and the Olive-tree, are Lunary. Also the Hearb [herb] Chinosta, which increaseth, and decreaseth with the Moon, viz. in substance, and number of leaves, not only in Sap, and vertue, which indeed is in some sort common to all Plants, except Onions, which are under the influence of Mars, which have contrary properties; As amongst flying things the Saturnine bird, called a

Quaile is a great enemy to the Moon and Sun. Lunary Animals are such as delight to be in mans company, and such as do naturally excell in love, or hatred, as all kinds of Dogs: The Chameleon also is Lunary, which alwaies assumes a colour according to the variety of the colour of the object: as the Moon changeth her nature according to the variety of the Signe which it is found in. Lunary also are Swine, Hinds, Goats, and all Animals whatsoever, that observe, and imitate the motion of the Moon: As the Baboon, and Panther, which is said to have a spot upon her shoulder like the Moon, increasing into a roundness, and having horns that bend inwards. Cats also are Lunary, whose eyes become greater or less, according to the course of the Moon: and those things which are of like nature, as Menstruous blood, of which are made wonderfull and strange things by Magicians; The Civet-Cat also changing her sex, being obnoxious to divers Sorceries, and all Animals that live in water as well as on land: as Otters, and such as prey upon fish. Also all Monstrous beasts, such as without any manifest seed are equivocally generated, as Mice, which sometimes are generated by Coition, sometimes of the putrefaction of the Earth. Amongst fowle, Geese, Ducks, Didoppers, and all kind of watery fowl as prey upon fish, as the Heron, and those that are equivocally produced, as Wasps of the Carkases [carcasses] of horses: Bees of the putrefaction of Cows, small Flies of putrefied wine, and Betles [beetles] of the flesh of Asses; but most Lunary of all is the two-horned Betle [beetle], horned after the manner of a Bull: which digs under Cow-dung, and there remaines for the space of twenty eight daies, in which time the Moon measures the whole Zodiack, and in the twenty ninth day, when it thinks there will be a conjunction of their brightness, it opens the dung and casts it into Water, from whence then come Betles [beetles]. Amongst fish these are Lunary, Ælurus, whose eyes are changed according to the course of the Moon, and whatsoever observes the motion of the Moon, as the Tortoise, the Echeneis, Crabs, Oisters [oysters], Cockles, and Frogs.

Chapter xxv. What things are Saturnine, or under the power of Saturne.

Saturnine things, amongst Elements, are Earth, and also Water: amongst humors, black Choller [choler] that is moist, as well natural, as adventitious, adust Choller [choler] excepted. Amongst tasts [tastes], soure, tart, and dead. Amongst Metals, Lead, and Gold, by reason of its weight, and the golden Marcasite. Amongst stones, the Onix [onyx], the Ziazaa, the Camonius, the Saphir [sapphire], the brown Jasper, the Chalcedon, the Loadstone, and all dark, weighty, earthy things. Amongst Plants, and Trees the Daffodill, Dragon-wort [drsgon's wort], Rue, Cummin [cumin], Hellebor [Hellebore], the tree from whence Benzoine comes, Mandrake, Opium, and those things which stupifie, and those things which are never sown, and never bear fruit, and those which bring forth berries of a dark colour, and black fruit, as the black Fig-tree, the Pine-tree, the Cypress-tree, and a certain tree used at burials, which never springs afresh with berries, rough, of a bitter tast [taste], of a strong smell, of a black shadow, yielding a most sharp pitch, bearing a most unprofitable fruit, never dies with age, deadly, dedicated to Pluto, as is the Hearb [herb] pas-flower, with which they were wont Anciently to strow the graves before they put the dead bodies into them, wherefore it was lawfull to make their Garlands at feasts with all Hearbs [herbs], and Flowers besides pas-flowers, because it was mournfull, and not conducing to mirth. Also all creeping Animals, living apart, and soli-tary, nightly, sad, contemplative, dull, covetous, fearfull, melancholly [melancholy], that take much pains, slow, that feed grosly, and such as eat their young. Of these kinds therefore are the Ape, the Cat, the Hog, the Mule, the Camel, the Bear, the Mole, the Asses, the Wolf, the Hare, the Dragon, the Basilisk, the Toad, all Serpents, and creep-ing things, Scorpions, Pismires [ants], and such things as proceed from putrefaction in the Earth, in Water, or in the ruines of houses, as Mice, and many sorts of Vermin. Amongst birds those are Satur-nine, which have long necks, and harsh voices, as Cranes, Estriches [ostriches], and Peacocks, which are dedicated to Saturn, and Juno. Also the scrich-Owle [screech-owl], the horn- Owle [horned-owl], the Bat, the Lapwing, the Crow, the Quaile, which is the most envious bird of all. Amongst fishes, the Eel, living apart from all other fish; the Lamprey, the Dog-fish, which devours her young, also the Tortoise, Oisters [oysters], Cockles, to which may be added Sea-spunges [sea-sponges], and all such things as come of them.

Chapter xxvi. What things are under the power of Jupiter, and are called Jovial.

Things under Jupiter, amongst Elements, are the Aire: amongst humors, blood, and the spirit of life, also all things which respect the encrease [increase], nourishment, and vegetation of the life. Amongst tasts [tastes] such as are sweet, and pleasant. Amongst Metals, Tin, Silver, and Gold, by reason of their temperateness: Amongst stones, the Hyacinth, Beril [beryl], Saphir [sapphire], the Emrald [emerald], green Jasper, and aiery colours: Amongst Plants and Trees, Sea-green, Garden Basil, Bugloss, Mace, Spike, Mints, Mastick, Elicampane, the Violet, Darnell, Henbane, the Poplar tree, and those which are called lucky trees, as the Oke [oak], the tree æsculus [horse-chestnut] which is like an Oke [oak] but much bigger, the Holm tree, the Beech tree, the Hasle [hazel] tree, the Service tree, the white Fig tree, the Pear tree, the Apple tree, the Vine, the Plum tree, the Ash, the Dog-tree, and the Olive tree, and also Oile. Also all manner of Corn, as Barley, Wheat, also Raisins, Licorish [licorice], Sugar, and all such things whose sweetness is manifest, and subtile, partaking somewhat of an astringent, and sharp tast [taste], as are Nuts, Almonds, Pine-apples [pineapples], Filberds [filberts], Pistake Nuts [pistachios], roots of Peony, Mirabolaus, Rhubarb, and Manna, Orpheus adds Storax.

Amongst Animals such as have some stateliness, and wisdom in them, and those which are mild, well trained up, and of good dispositions, as the Hart and Elephant, and those which are gentle, as Sheep and Lambs: Amongst birds, those that are of a temperate complexion, as

Hens, together with the Yolk of their Eggs. Also the Partridge, the Pheasant, the Swallow, the Pellican [pelican], the Cuckow [cuckoo], the Stork, birds given to a kind of devotion which are Emblemes of gratitude. The Eagle is dedicated to Jupiter, she is the Ensigne of Emperours, and an Embleme of Justice, and Clemency.

Amongst fish, the Dolphin, the fish called Anchia [anchovy], the Sheath fish, by reason of his devoutness.

Chapter xxvii. What things are under the power of Mars, and are called Martial.

These things are Martiall, amongst Elements, Fire, together with all adust, and sharp things: Amongst humours, Choller [choler]; also bitter tasts [tastes], tart, and burning the tongue, and causing tears: Amongst Metals, Iron, and red Brass; and all fiery, red, and sulphureous things: Amongst Stones the Diamond, Loadstone, the Bloodstone [bloodstone], the Jasper, the stone that consists of divers kinds, and the Amethist [amethyst]. Amongst Plants, and Trees, Hellebor, Garlick, Euphorbium, Cartabana, Armoniack, Radish, the Laurell, Wolfs-bane [wolfsbane], Scammony, and all such as are poysonous [poisonous], by reason of too much heat, and those which are beset round about with prickles, or by touching the skin, burn it, prick it, or make it swell, as Cardis, the Nettle, Crow-foot, and such as being eaten cause tears, as Onyons [onions], Ascolonia, Leeks, Mustard-seed, and all thorny Trees, and the Dog-tree, which is dedicated to Mars. And all such Animals as are warlike, ravenous, bold, and of clear fancy, as the Horse, Mule, Goat, Kid, Wolf, Libard [leopard], the wild Ass; Serpents also, and Dragons full of displeasure and poyson [poison]; also all such as are offensive to men, as Gnats, Flies, Baboon, by reason of his anger. All birds that are ravenous, devour flesh, break bones, as the Eagle, the Faulcon [falcon], the Hawk, the Vultur [vulture]; and those which are called the fatall Birds, as the Horn-Owl, the Scrich-Owl [screech-owl], Castrels, Kites, and such as are hungry, and ravenous, and such as make a noise in their swallowing, as

Crows, Daws, the Pie, which above all the rest is dedicated to Mars. And amongst Fishes, the Pike, the Barbell, the Fork-fish, the Fish that hath horns like a Ram, the Sturgeon, the Glacus, all which are great devourers, and ravenous.

Chapter xxviii. What things are under the power of Venus, and are called Venereall.

These things are under Venus, amongst Elements, Aire, and Water; amongst humours, Flegm [phlegm], with Blood, Spirit, and Seed; amongst tasts [tastes], those which are sweet, unctuous, and delectable; amongst Metals, Silver, and Brass, both yellow, and red; amongst Stones, the Berill [beryl], Chrysolite, Emrald [emerald], Saphir [sapphire], green Jasper, Corneola [carnelian], the stone Aetites, the Lazull [lazuli] stone, Corall, and all of a fair, various, white, and green Colour; amongst Plants and Trees the Vervin [vervain], Violet, Maidenhaire, Valerian, which by the Arabian is called Phu; also Thyme, the gum Ladanum, Amber-grise [ambergris], Musk, Sanders [sandalwood], Coriander, and all sweet perfumes, and delightfull, and sweet fruits, as sweet Pears, Figs, Pomegranats [pomegranates], which the Poets say was, in Cyprus, first sown by Venus. Also the Rose of Lucifer was dedicated to her, also the Myrtle tree of Hesperus. Moreover all luxurious, delicious Animals, and of a strong love, as Dogs, Conies, stinking Sheep, and Goats, both female, and male, which generates sooner then any other Animall, for they say that he couples after the seventh day of his being brought forth; also the Bull for his disdain, and the Calf for his wantonness. Amongst birds the Swan, the Wagtail, the Swallow, the Pellican [pelican], the Burgander, which are very loving to their yong [young]. Also the Crow, and Pigeon, which is dedicated to Venus, and the Turtle [turtledove], one whereof was Commanded to be offered at the purification, after bringing forth. The Sparrow also was dedicated to Venus, which was Commanded in the Law to be used in the purification, after the Leprosie [leprosy], a martiall disease, then which nothing was of more force to resist it. Also the Egyptians called the Eagle Venus, because she is prone to Venery, for after she hath been trod thirteen times a day, if the Male call her, she runs to him again.

Amongst fishes, these are Venereall, the lustfull Pilchards, the letcherous [lecherous] Gilthead, the Whiting for her love to her yong [young], Crab fighting for his Mate, and Tithymallus for its fragrance, and sweet smell.

Chapter xxix. What things are under the power of Mercury, and are called Mercuriall.

Things under Mercury are these; amongst Elements, Water, although it moves all things indistinctly; amongst humors, those especially which are mixed, as also the Animall spirit; amongst tasts [tastes] those that are various, strange, and mixed: amongst Metals, Quicksilver, Tin, the Slver Marcasite; amongst stones, the Emrald [emerald], Achates [agates], red Marble, Topaze, and those which are of divers colours, and various figures naturally, & those that are artificiall, as glass, & those which have a colour mixed with yellow, and green. Amongst Plants, and Trees, the Hazle [hazel], Five-leaved-grass, the Hearb [herb] Mercury, Fumitary, Pimpernell, Marjoram, Parsly [parsley], and such as have shorter and less leaves, being compounded of mixed natures, and divers colours. Animals also, that are of quick sence, ingenious, strong, inconstant, swift, and such as become easily acquainted with men, as Dogs, Apes, Foxes, Weesels [weasels], the Hart, and Mule; and all Animals that are of both sexes, and those which can change their Sex, as the Hare, Civet-Cat, and such like. Amongst birds, those which are naturally witty, melodious, and inconstant, as the Linet, Nightingale, Blackbird, Thrush, Lark, the Gnat- sapper, the bird Calandra, the Parret [parrot], the Pie, the Bird Ibis, the bird Porphyrio, the black Betle [beetle] with one horn. And amongst fish, the fish called Trochius, which goes into himself, also Pourcontrell for deceitfulness, and changeableness, and the Fork fish for its industry; the Mullet also that shakes off the bait on the hook with his taile.

Chapter xxx. That the whole sublunary World, and those things which are in it, are distributed to Planets.

Moreover whatsoever is found in the whole world is made according to the governments of the Planets, and accordingly receives its vertue. So in Fire the enlivening light thereof is under the government of the Sun, the heat of it under Mars, in the Earth, the various superficies thereof under the Moon, and Mercury; and the starry Heaven, the whole mass of it under Saturne, but in the middle Elements, Aire is under Jupiter, and Water the Moon, but being mixed are under Mercury, and Venus. In like manner naturall active causes observe the Sun, the matter the Moon, the fruitfulness of active causes Jupiter, the fruitfullness of the matter, Venus, the sudden effecting of any thing, Mars, and Mercury, that for his vehemency, this for his dexterity, and manifold vertue: But the permanent continuation of all things is ascribed to Saturne. Also amongst Vegetables, every thing that bears fruit is from Jupiter, and every thing that bears Flowers is from Venus, all Seed, and Bark is from Mercury, and all roots from Saturne, and all Wood from Mars, and leaves from the Moon. Wherefore, all that bring forth fruit, and not Flowers, are of Saturne and Jupiter, but they that bring forth Flowers, and Seed, and not fruit, are of Venus, and Mercury; These which are brought forth of their own accord without Seed, are of the Moon, and Saturn; All beauty is from Venus, all strength from Mars, and every Planet rules, and disposeth that which is like to it. Also in stones, their weight, Clamminess, and Sliptickness is of Saturne, their use, and temperament of Jupiter, their hardness from Mars, their life from the Sun, their beauty and fairness from Venus, their occult vertue from Mercury, and their common use from the Moon.

4

Section 4

C hapter xxxi. How Provinces, and Kingdomes are distributed to Planets.

Moreover the whole Orb of the Earth is distributed by Kingdoms, and Provinces to the Planets, and Signes: For Macedonia, Thracia, Illyria, Arriana, Gordiana, (many of which countries are in the lesser Asia) are under Saturne with Capricorn; but with Aquarius, under him are the Sauromatian Country, Oxiana, Sogdiana, Arabia, Phazania, Media and Æthiopia [Ethiopia], which Countries for the most part belong to the more inward Asia. Under Jupiter with Sagittarius are Tuscana, Celtica, Spaine, and happy Arabia: under him with Pisces, are Lycia, Lydia, Cilicia, Pamphylia, Paphlagonia, Nasamonia, and Lybia. Mars with Aries governs Britany, France, Germany, Bastarnia, the lower parts of Syria, Idumea, and Judea: with Scorpio, he rules Syria, Comagena, Cappadocia, Metagonium, Mauritania, and Getulia. The Sun with Leo governs Italy, Apulia, Sicilia, Phenicia, Chaldea, & the Orchenians. Venus with Taurus governs the Isles Cyclades, the Seas of litle Asia, Cyprus, Parthia, Media, Persia: but with Libra she commands the people of the Island Bractia, of Caspia, of Seres, of Thebais, of Oasis, and of Troglodys. Mercury with Gemini, rules Hircania, Armenia, Mantiana, Cyrenaica, Marmarica, and the lower Egypt: but with Virgo, Greece, Achaia, Creta, Babylon, Mesopotamia, Assyria, and Ela, whence they of that place are in Scripture called Elamites. The Moon with Cancer governs Bithivia, Phrygia, Colchica, Numidia, Africa, Carthage, and all Carchedonia.

These we have in this manner gathered from Ptolemies [Ptolemy's] opinion, to which according to the writings of other Astrologers many more may be added. But he which knows how to compare these divisions of Provinces according to the divisions of the Stars, with the Ministery [Ministry] of the ruling Intelligencies, and blessings of the Tribes of Israel, the lots of the Apostles, and typicall seales of the sacred Scripture, shall be able to obtain great and propheticall oracles concerning every Region, of things to come.

Chapter xxxii. What things are under the Signes, the fixed Stars, and their Images.

The like consideration is to be had in all things concerning the figures of the fixed Stars: so they will have the Terrestiall [terrestrial] Ram to be under the rule of the Celestiall Aries: and the Terrestiall Bull, and Ox to be under the Celestiall Taurus. So also that Cancer should rule over Crabs, and Leo over Lyons [lions]: Virgo over Virgins, and Scorpio over Scorpions. Capricorn over Goats. Sagittarius over Horses, and Pisces over Fishes. Also the Celestiall Ursa over Bears, Hydra over Serpents, and the Dog-star over Dogs, and so of the rest. Now Apuleius distributes certain and peculiar Hearbs [herbs] to the Signes, and Planets, viz. To Aries the Hearb [herb] Sange [sage], to Taurus Vervine [vervain] that growes straight, to Gemini Vervine [vervain] that growes bending, to Cancer Comfrey, to Leo Sowbread, to Virgo Calamint, to Libra Mug-wort, to Scorpio Scorpion-grass, to Sagittarius Pimpernell, to Capricorn the Dock, to Aquarius Dragon- wort [dragon's-wort], to Pisces Hart-wort. And to the Planets these, viz. to Saturne Sen- green, to Jupiter Agrimony, to Mars Sulphur-wort, to the Sun Marygold [marigold], to Venus Wound-wort, to Mercury Mulleine, to the Moon, Peony. But Hermes, whom Albertus follows, distributes to the Planets these, viz. to Saturne the Daffodill, to Jupiter Henbane, to Mars Rib-wort, to the Sun Knotgrass, to Venus Vervine [vervain], to Mercury Cinquefoile, to the Moon, Goos-foot. We also know by experience that Asparagus is under Aries, and Garden-basill under Scorpio; For of the shavings of Rams- horn sowed, comes forth Asparagus, and Garden Basill rubbed betwixt two stones, produceth Scorpions. Moreover I will according to the doctrine of Hermes, and Thebit reckon up some of the more eminent Stars, whereof the first is called the head of Algol, and amongst stones, rules over the Diamond, amongst Plants, black Hellebor, and Mugwort. The second are the Pleiades, or seven Stars, which amongst stones, rule over Crystall, and the stone Diodocus; amongst Plants, the Hearb [herb] Diacedon, and Frankincense, and Fennill [fennel]: and amongst Metals, Quicksilver [quicksilver]. The third is the Star Aldeboran, which hath under it, amongst stones, the Carbuncle, and Ruby: amongst Plants, the Milky Thistle, and Matry-silva. The fourth is called the Goat- Star, which rules, amongst stones, the Saphir [sapphire], amongst Plants, Horehound, Mint, Mugwort, and Mandrake. The fifth is called the great Dog-star, which amongst stones, rules over the Berill [beryl]: amongst Plants, Savin, Mugwort and Dragonwort: and amongst Animals the tongue of a Snake. The sixth is called the lesser Dog-star, and, amongst stones, rules over Achates [agates]: amongst Plants the Flowers of Marigold, and Penyroial [pennyroyal]. The seventh is called the Heart of the Lyon, which amongst stones, rules over the Granate; amongst Plants, Sallendine, Mugwort, and Mastick. The eighth is the Taile of the lesser Bear, which amongst stones, rules over the Loadstone, amongst Hearbs [herbs], Succory, whose leaves, and Flowers turn towards the North, also Mugwort, and the flowers of Perwinckle [periwinkle]; and amongst Animals the tooth of a Wolf. The ninth is called the Wing of the Crow, under which, amongst stones, are such stones as are of the Colour of the black Onyx stone: amongst Plants the Bur, Quadraginus, Henbane, and Comfrey; and amongst Animals the tongue of a Frog. The tenth is called Spica, which hath under it, amongst stones, the Emrald [emerald]: amongst Plants, Sage, Trifoile, Perwinkle [periwinkle], Mugwort, and Mandrake. The eleventh is called Alchamech, which amongst stones, rules over the Jasper: amongst Plants the Plantain. The twelfth is called

Elpheia, under this, amongst stones, is the Topaze; amongst Plants, Rosemary, Trifoile, and Ivy. The thirteenth is called the Heart of the Scorpion, under which, amongst stones, is the Sardonius, and Amethist [amethyst]; amongst Plants long Aristolochy, and Saffron. The fourteenth is the Falling Vultur, under which, amongst stones, is the Chrysolite: amongst Plants Succory, and Fumitary. The fifteenth is the Taile of Capricorn under which, amongst stones, is the Chalcedone [chalcedony]: amongst Plants, Majoram [marjoram], Mugwort, and Nip [catnip], and the root of Mandrake.

Moreover this we must know, that every stone, or Plant, or Animall, or any other thing, is not governed by one Star alone, but many of them receive influence, not separated, but conjoyned, from many Stars. So amongst stones, the Chalcedony is under Saturne, and Mercury, together with the Taile of Scorpion, and Capricorn. The Saphir [sapphire] under Jupiter, Saturne, and the Star Alhajoth; Tutia is under Jupiter, and the Sun and Moon, the Emrald [emerald] under Jupiter, Venus, and Mercury, and the Star Spica. The Amethyst, as saith Hermes, is under Mars, Jupiter, and the Heart of the Scorpion. The Jasper, which is of divers kinds is under Mars, Jupiter, and the Star Alchamech, the Chrysolite is under the Sun, Venus, and Mercury, as also under the Star which is called the falling Vultur; the Topaze under the Sun, and the Star Elpheia: the Diamond under Mars, and the Head of Algol. In like manner amongst Vegetables, the Hearb [herb] Dragon is under Saturne, and the Celestiall Dragon, Mastick, and Mints, are under Jupiter, and the Sun; but Mastick is also under the Heart of the Lyon, and Mint under the Goat star: Hellebor is dedicated to Mars, and the Head of Algol, Mosse, and Sanders, to the Sun, and Venus: Coriander to Venus, and Saturne. Amongst Animals, the Sea Calf is under the Sun, and Jupiter; The Fox, and Ape under Saturne, and Mercury: and Domesticall Dogs under Mercury, and the Moon. And thus we have shewed more things in these inferiours by their superiours.

Chapter xxxiii. Of the Seals, and Characters of Naturall things.
All Stars have their peculiar Natures, properties, and conditions, the
Seals and Characters whereof they produce through their rayes, even
in these inferiour things, viz. in Elements, in Stones, in Plants, in
Animals, and their members, whence every thing receives from an
harmonious disposition, and from its Star shining upon it, some particular Seal, or Character stampt upon it, which is the significator of
that Star, or harmony, conteining in it a peculiar vertue, differing
from other vertues of the same matter, both generically, specifically,
and numerically. Every thing therefore hath its Character pressed
upon it by its Star for some particular effect, especially by that Star
which doth principally govern it: And these Characters contain, and
retain in them the peculiar natures, vertues, and roots of their Stars,
and produce the like operations upon other things, on which they are
reflected, and stir up, and help the influencies of their Stars, whether
they be Planets, or fixed Stars, and figures, and Celestiall signs, viz. as
oft as they shall be made in a fit matter, and in their due, and accustomed times. Which ancient wise men considering, such as laboured
much in the finding out of the occult properties of things, did set
down in writing the images of the Stars, their figures, Seals, Marks,
Characters, such as nature her self did describe by the rayes of the
Stars, in these inferiour bodies, some in stones, some in Plants, and
joynts, and knots of boughs, and some in divers members of Animals.
For the Bay-tree, the Lote-tree, and the Marygold [marigold] are Solary Plants, and in their roots, and knots being cut off, shew the Characters of the Sun, so also in the bone, and shoulderblades in Animals:
whence there arose a spatulary kind of divining (i.e.) by the shoul-
der-blades, and in stones, and stony things the Characters, and images
of Celestiall things are often found. But seeing that in so great a diversity of things there is not a traditionall knowledge, only in a few
things, which humane understanding is able to reach: Therefore leav-
ing those things which are to be found out in Plants, and Stones, and
other things, as also, in the members of divers Animals, we shall limit

our selves to mans nature only, which seeing it is the compleatest image of the whole universe, containing in it self the whole heavenly harmony, will without all doubt abundantly afford us the Seals, and Characters of all the Stars, and Celestiall Influencies, and those as the more efficacious, which are less differing from the Celestiall nature. But as the number of the Stars is known to God alone, so also their effects, and Seals upon these inferiour things: wherefore no humane intellect is able to attain to the knowledge of them. Whence very few of those things became known to us, which the ancient Philosophers, & Chyromancers [chiromancers] attained to, partly by reason, and partly by experience, and there be many things yet ly hid in the treasury of nture. We shall here in this place note some few Seals,and Characters of the Planets, such as the ancient Chyromancers [chiromancers] knew in the hands of men. These doth Julian call sacred, and divine letters, seeing that by them, according to the holy Scripture is the life of men writ in their hands. And there are in all Nations, and Languages alwaies the same, and like to them, and permanent; to which were added, and found out afterwards many more, as by the ancient, so by latter Chyromancers [chiromancers]. And they that would know them must have recourse to their Volumes. It is sufficient here to shew from whence the Characters of Nature have their originall, and in what things they are to be enquired after.

There follow the Figures of Divine Letters.

The Letters, or Characters of Saturne.

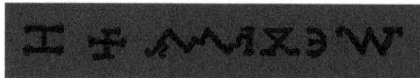

The Letters, or Characters of Jupiter.

The Letters, or Characters of Mars.

The Letters, or Characters of the Sun.

The Letters, or Characters of Venus.

The Letters, or Characters of Mercury.

The Letters, or Characters of the Moon.

Chapter xxxiv. How by Naturall things, and their vertues we may draw forth, and attract the influencies, and vertues of Celestiall bodies.

Now if thou desirest to receive vertue from any part of the World, or from any Star, thou shalt (those things being used which belong to this Star) come under its peculiar influence, as Wood is fit to receive Flame, by reason of Sulphur, Pitch, and Oile.

Nevertheless when thou dost to any one species of things, or individual, rightly apply many things, which are things of the same subject scattered amongst themselves, conformable to the same Idea, and Star, presently by this matter so opportunely fitted, a singular gift is infused by the Idea, by means of the soul of the world. I say opportunely fitted, viz. under a harmony like to the harmony, which did infuse a certain vertue into the matter. For although things have some vertues, such as we speak of, yet those vertues do so ly [lie] hid that there is seldom any effect produced by them: but as in a grain of Mustardseed, bruised, the sharpness which lay hid is stirred up: and as the heat of the fire doth make letters apparently seen, which before could not be read, that were writ with the juice of an Onion or milk: and letters wrote upon a stone with the fat of a Goat, and altogether unperceived, when the stone is put into Vinegar, appear and shew themselves. And as a blow with a stick stirs up the madness of a Dog, which before lay asleep, so doth the Celestiall harmony disclose vertues lying in the water, stirs them up, strengtheneth them, and makes them manifest, and as I may so say, produceth that into Act, which before was only in power, when things are rightly exposed to it in a Celestiall season. As for example; If thou dost desire to attract vertue from the Sun, and to seek those things that are Solary, amongst Vegetables, Plants, Metals, Stones, and Animals, these things are to be used, and taken chiefly, which in a Solary order are higher. For these are more available: So thou shalt draw a singular gift from the Sun through the beams thereof, being seasonably received together, and through the spirit of the world.

Chapter xxxv. Of the Mixtions of naturall things, one with another, and their benefits.

It is most evident, that in the inferiour nature all the powers of superior bodies are not found comprehended in any one thing, but are dispersed through many kinds of things amongst us: as there are many Solary things, whereof every one doth not contain all the vertues of the Sun: but some have some properties from the Sun, and others othersome. Wherefore it is sometimes necessary that there be mixtions in operations, that if a hundred or a thousand vertues of the Sun were dispersed through so many Plants, Animals, & the like, we may gather all these together, and bring them into one form, in which we shall see all the said vertues, being united, contained. Now there is a twofold vertue in commixtion, one, viz. which was first planted in its parts, and is Celestiall, the other is obtained by a certain, and artificiall mixtion of things mixt amongst themselves, and of the mixtions of them according to certain proportions, such as agree with the heaven under a certain Constellation; And this vertue descends by a certain likeness, and aptness that is in things amongst themselves towards their superiours, and just as much as the following do by degrees correspond with them that go before, where the patient is fitly applyed to its agent. So from a certain composition of Hearbs [herbs], vapours, and such like, made according to naturall Philosophy, and Astronomy, there results a certain common form, endowed with many gifts of the Stars: as in the honey of Bees, that which is gathered out of the juice of innumerable Flowers, and brought into one form, contains the vertue of all, by a kind of divine, and admirable art of the Bees. Yet this is not to be less wondred at which Eudoxus Giudius reports of an artificiall kind of honey, which a certain Nation of Gyants [giants] in Lybia knew how to make out of Flowers, and that very good, and not far inferiour to that of the Bees. For every mixtion, which consists of many severall things, is then most perfect, when it is so firmly compacted in all parts, that it becomes one, is every where firm to it self, and can hardly be dissipated: as we sometimes see stones, and divers bodies to be by a certain naturall power conglutinated, and united, that they seem to be wholly one thing: as we see two trees by grafting to become one, also Oisters [oysters] with stones by a certain occult vertue of nature, and there have been seen some Animals which have been turned into stones, and so united with the substance of the stone, that they seem to make one body, and that also homogeneous. So the tree Ebeny [ebony] is one while wood, and another while stone.

When therefore any one makes a mixtion of many matters under the Celestiall influencies, then the variety of Celestiall actions on the one hand, and of naturall powers on the other hand, being joyned together doth indeed cause wonderfull thing, by ointments, by collyries, by fumes, and such like, which viz. are read in the book of Chiramis, Archyta, Democritus, and Hermes, who is named Alchorat, and of many others.

Chapter xxxvi. Of the Union of mixt things, and the introduction of a more noble form, and the Senses of life.

Moreover we must know, that by how much the more noble the form of any thing is, by so much the more prone, and apt it is to receive, and powerfull to act. Then the vertues of things do then become wonderfull, viz. when they are put to matters that are mixed, and prepared in fit seasons, to make them alive, by procuring life for them from the Stars, as also a sensible soul, as a more noble form. For there is so great a power in prepared matters which we see do then receive life, when a perfect mixtion of qualities seems to break the former contrariety. For so much the more perfect life things receive, by how much their temper is more remote from contrariety. Now the Heaven, as a prevalent cause doth from the beginning of every thing to be generated by the concoction, and perfect digestion of the matter, together with life, bestows Celestiall influences, and wonderfull gifts, according to the Capacity that is in that life, and sensible soul to receive more noble, and sublime vertues. For the Celestiall vertue doth otherwise lye asleep, as Sulphur kept from Flame, but in living bodies it doth alwaies burn, as kindled Sulphur, then by its vapour it fils all the places that are next to it; so certain wonderfull works are wrought, such as are read of in the book of Nemith, which is tituled a Book of the Laws of Pluto, because such kind of monstrous generations are not produced according to the Laws of Nature. For we know that of Worms are generated Gnats, of a Horse Waspes, of a Calf, and Ox Bees, of a Crab, his legs being taken of [off], and he buried in the ground, a Scorpion; of a Duck dryed into powder, and put into Water, are generated Frogs; but if it be baked in a Pie, and cut into pieces, and put into a moist place under the ground, Toads are generated of it: of the Hearb [herb] Garden Basill bruised betwixt two stones, are generated Scorpions, and of the hairs of a menstrous Woman put under dung, are bred Serpents; and the hair of a Horse taile put into Water, receiveth life, and is turned into a pernicious Worm. And there is an art wherewith by a Hen sitting upon Eggs may be generated a form like to a man, which I have seen, & knww how to make, which Magicians say hath in it wonderfull vertues, and this they call the true Mandrake. You must therefore know which, and what kind of matters are either of nature, or art, begun, or perfected, or compounded of more things, and what Celestiall influencies they are able to receive. For a Congruity of naturall things is sufficient for the receiving of influence from Celestiall; because when nothing doth hinder the Celestials to send forth their lights upon inferiours, they suffer no matter to be destitute of their vertue. Wherefore as much matter as is perfect, and pure, is not unfit to receive the Celestiall influence. For that is the binding and continuity of the matter to the soul of the world, which doth so daily flow in upon things naturall, and all things which nature hath prepared, that it is impossible that a prepared matter should not receive life, or a more noble form.

Chapter xxxvii. How by some certain naturall, and artificiall preparations we may attract certain Celestiall, and vitall Gifts.
Platonists, together with Hermes, say, and Jarchus Brachmanus, and the Mecubals of the Hebrews confess, that all sublunary things are subject to generation, and corruption, and that also there are the same things in the Celestiall world, but after a Celestiall manner, as also in the intellectuall world, but in a far more perfect, and better fashion, and manner, but in the most perfect manner of all in the exemplary. And after this course, that every inferiour thing should in its kind answer its superiour, and through this the supream [Supreme] it self, and receive from heaven that Celestiall power they call the quintessence, or the spirit of the world, or the middle nature, and from the intellectuall world a spirituall and enlivening vertue transcending all qualities whatsoever, and lastly from the exemplary or originall world, through the mediation of the other, according to their degree receive the originall power of the whole perfection. Hence

every thing may be aptly reduced from these inferiours to the Stars, from the Stars to their Intelligencies, and from thence to the first cause it self; from the series, and order whereof whole Magick, and all occult Philosophy flowes: For every day some naturall thing is drawn by art, and some divine thing is drawn by nature, which the Egyptians seeing, called Nature a Magicianess, (i.e.) the very Magicall power it self, in the attracting of like by like, and of sutable things by sutable. Now such kind of attractions by the mutuall correspondency of things amongst themselves, of superiours with inferiours, the Grecians called συμπαθιαν [sympathies]. So the earth agrees with cold water, the water with moist Aire, the Aire with Fire, the Fire with the Heaven in water; neither is Fire mixed with water, but by Aire, nor the Aire with the Earth, but by water. So neither is the soul united to the body, but by the spirit, nor the understanding to the spirit but by the soul. So we see that when nature hath framed the body of an infant, by this very preparative she presently fetcheth the spirit from the Universe. This spirit is the instrument to obtain of God the understanding, and mind in the soul, and body, as in wood the dryness is fitted to receive oile, and the oile being imbibed is food for the Fire, the Fire is the vehiculum of light. By these examples you see how by some certain naturall, and artificiall preparations, we are in a capacity to receive certain Celestiall gifts from above. For stones, and Metals have a correspondency with Hearbs [herbs], Hearbs [herbs] with Animals, Animals with the Heavens, the Heavens with Intelligencies, and those with divine properties, and attributes, and with God himself, after whose image, and likness all things are created.

Now the first Image of God is the world, of the world, man, of man, beasts, of beasts, the Zeophyton (i.e.) half Animall, and half Plant; of Zeophyton, plants, of plants, metals, of metals, stones. And again in things spirituall, the Plant agrees with a bruit [brute] in Vegetation, a bruit [brute] with a man in sense, man with an Angel in understanding, an Angell with God in immortality. Divinity is annexed to the mind, the mind to the intellect, the intellect to the intention, the intention to the imagination, the imagination to the senses, the senses at last to things. For this is the band, and continuity of nature, that all superior vertue doth flow through every inferiour with a long, and continued series, dispersing its rayes even to the very last things; and inferiours through their superiours, come to the very supream [Supreme] of all. For so inferiours are successively joyned to their superiours, that there proceeds an influence from their head, the first cause, as a certain string stretched out, to the lowermost things of all, of which string if one end be touched, the whole doth presently shake, and such a touch doth sound to the other end, and at the motion of the inferiour, the superiour also is moved, to which the other doth answer, as strings in a Lute well tuned.

Chapter xxxviii. How we may draw not only Celestiall, and vitall, but also certain Intellectuall, and divine gifts from above.

Magicians teach that Celestial gifts may through inferiors being conformable to superiors be drawn down by opportune influencies of the Heaven; and so also by these Celestial [gifts], the Celestial Angels, as they are servants of the Stars, may be procured, and conveyed to us. Iamblichus, Proclus, and Synesius, with the whole School of Platonists confirm, that not only Celestiall, and vitall, but also certain Intellectuall, Angelicall, and divine gifts may be received from above by some certain matters, having a naturall power of divinity (i.e.) which have a naturall correspondency with the superiors, being rightly received, and opportunely gathered together according to the rules of Naturall Philosophy, and Astronomy: And Mercurius Trismegistus writes, that an Image rightly made of certain proper things, appropriated to any one certain Angel, will presently be animated by that Angel. Of the same also Austin [St. Augustine] makes mention in his eighth book De Civitate Dei [the City of God]. For this is the harmony of the world, that things supercelestiall be drawn down by the Celestiall, and the super-naturall [supernatural] by naturall, because there is one operative vertue that is diffused through all kinds of things, by which vertue indeed, as manifest things are produced out of occult causes; so a Magician doth make use of things manifest, to draw forth things that are occult, viz. through the rays of the Stars, through fumes, lights, sounds, and naturall things, which are agreeable to Celestiall: in which, besides corporeall qualities, there is a kind of reason, sense, and harmony, and incorporeall, and divine measures, and orders. So we read that the Ancients were wont often to receive some divine, and wonderfull thing by certain naturall things: so the stone that is bred in the Apple of the eye of a Civet Cat, held under the tongue of a man, is said to make him to divine, or prophesie [prophesy]: The same is Selenite, the Moon stone [moonstone], reported to do, so they say that the Images of Gods may be called up by the stone called Anchitis, and that the Ghosts of the dead may be, being called up, kept up by the stone Synochitis. The like doth the Hearb [herb] Aglauphotis do, which is called Marmorites, growing upon the Marbles of Arabia, as saith Pliny, and the which Magicians use. Also there is an Hearb [herb] called Rheangelida, which Magicians drinking of, can prophesie [prophesy].

Moreover there are some Hearbs [herbs] by which the dead are raised to life; whence Xanthus the Historian tels, that with a certain Hearb [herb] called Balus, a young Dragon being killed, was made alive again, also that by the same a certain man of Tillum, whom a Dragon killed, was restored to life: and Juba reports, that in Arabia a certain man was by a certain Hearb [herb] restored to life. But whether or no any such things can be done indeed upon man by the vertue of Hearbs [herbs], or any other naturall thing, we shall discourse in the following Chapter. Now it is certain, and manifest that such things can be done upon other animals. So if flies, that are drowned, be put into warm ashes, they revive. And Bees being drowned, do in like manner recover life in the juice of the hearb Nip [herb catnip]; and Eels being dead for want of water, if with their whole bodies they be put under mud in vineger [vinegar], and the blood of a Vultur [vulture] being put to them, will all of them in a few dayes recover life. They say that if the fish Echeneis be cut into peices [pieces], and cast into the sea, the parts will within a little time come together, and live. Also we know that the Pellican [pelican] doth restore her yong [young] to life, being killed, with her own blood.

Chap. xxxix. That we may by some certain matters of the world stir up the Gods of the world, and their ministring spirits.

No man is ignorant that evill spirits, by evill, and prophane [profane] Arts may be raised up as Psellus saith Sorcerers are wont to do, whom most detestable and abominable filthiness did follow, and accompany, such as were in times past in the sacrifices of Priapus, and in the worship of the Idoll which was called Panor, to whom they did sacrifice with their privy members [genitals] uncovered. Neither to these is that unlike (if it be true, and not a fable) which is read concerning the detestable heresy of old Church- men, and like to these are manifest in Witches and mischeivous [mischievous] women, which wickednesses the foolish dotage of women is subject to fall into. By these, and such as these evill spirits are raised. As a wicked spirit spake once to Iohn [John] of one Cynops a Sorcerer; all the power, saith he, of Satan dwells there, and he is entred into a confederacy with all the principalities together, and likewise we, with him, and Cynops obeys us, and we again obey him. Again, on the contrary side, no man is ignorant that supercelestiall Angels or spirits may be gained by us through good works, a pure mind, secret prayers, devout humiliation, and the like. Let no man therefore doubt that in like manner by some certain matters of the world, the Gods of the world may be raised by us, or at least the ministring spirits, or servants of these Gods, and as Mercurius [Hermes Trismegistus] saith, the airy spirits, not supercelestiall, much less higher. So we read that the antient [ancient] Priests made statues, and images, foretelling things to come, and infused into them the spirits of the stars, which were not kept there by constraint in some certain matters, but rejoycing [rejoiced] in them, viz. as acknowledging such kinds of matter to be sutable [suitable] to them, they do alwaies and willingly abide in them, and speak, and do wonderfull things by them: no otherwise then evill spirits are wont to do, when they possess mens bodies.

Chap. xl. Of bindings, what sort they are of, and in what wayes they are wont to be done.

WEE have spoken concerning the vertues, and wonderfull efficacy of naturall things. It remains now that we understand a thing of great wonderment: and it is a binding of men into love, or hatred, sickness or health, and such like. Also the binding of thieves, and robbers, that they cannot steale in any place; the binding of Merchants, that they cannot buy, or sell in any place; the binding of an army, that they cannot pass over any bound; the binding of ships, that no winds, though never so strong, shall be able to carry them out of the Haven. Also the binding of a mill, that it can by no force whatsoever be turned round: the binding of a Cisterne, or fountain, that the water cannot be drawn up out of them: The binding of the ground, that it cannot bring forth fruit: the binding of any place, that nothing can be built upon it: The binding of fire, that though it be never so strong, can burn no combustible thing that is put to it. Also the bindings of lightnings, and tempests, that they shall do no hurt. The binding of dogs, that they cannot bark. Also the binding of birds, and wild beasts, that they shall not be able to fly, or run away. And such like as these, which are scarce credible, yet often known by experience. Now there are such kind of bindings as these made by Sorceries, Collyries, Unguents, love potions, by binding to, and hanging up of things, by rings, by charmes, by strong imaginations, and passions, by images, and characters, by inchantments [enchantments], and imprecations, by lights, by sound, by numbers, by words, and names, invocations, sacrifices, by swearing, conjuring, consecrations, devotions, and by divers superstitions, and observations, and such like.

5

Section 5

Chap. xli. Of Sorceries, and their power.

The force of Sorceries is reported to be so great, that they are believed to be able to subvert, consume, and change all inferiour things, according Virgils Muse.

Moeris for me these hearbs [herbs] in Pontus chose, And curious drugs, for there great plenty grows;

I many times, with these, have Moeris spide [spied] Chang'd to a wolfe, and in the woods to hide: From Sepulchres would souls departed charm,

And Corn bear standing from anothers Farm.

Also in an other place, concerning the companions of Ulysses, whom

The cruell Goddess Circe there invests

With fierce aspects, and chang'd to savage beasts.

And a litle after,

When love from Picus Circe could not gaine Him with her charming wand, and hellish bane Chang'd to a bird, and spots his speckled wings With sundry colours ----------

Now, there are some kinds of these sorceries mentioned by Lucan concerning that Sorceress Thessala, calling up ghosts, where he saith,

Here all natures products unfortunate;

Fomr [foam] of mad Dogs, which waters fear and hate; Guts of the Lynx; Hyena's knot imbred;

The marrow of a Hart with Serpents fed Were not wanting; no nor the sea Lamprey

Which stops the ships; nor yet the Dragons eye.

And such as Apuleius tells of concerning Pamphila, that Sorceress, endeavouring to procure love; to whom Fotis a certain maid brought the haires of a goat (cut off from a bag or botle [bottle] made with the skin thereof) instead of Bæotius a young mans haires: Now she (saith he) being out of her wits for the young man, goeth up to the tyled rough [tiled roof], and in the upper part thereof makes a great hole open to all the orientall, and other aspects, and most fit for these her arts, and there privately worships, having before furnished her mournfull house with sutable furniture, with all kinds of spices, with plates of Iron with strange words engraven upon them, with sterns of ships that were cast away, and much lamented, and with divers members of buryed carkasses [buried carcasses] cast abroad: here noses, and fingers, there the fleshy nailes of those that were hanged, and in another place the blood of them that were murdered, and their skulls mangled with the teeth of wild beasts; then she offers sacrifices (their inchanted entralls [enchanted entrails] lying panting), and sprinkles them with divers kinds of liquors; sometimes with fountain water, sometimes with cowes milk, sometimes with mountain honey, and mead: Then she ties those haires into knots, and layes them on the fire, with divers odours to be burnt. Then presently with an irresistible power of Magick, and blind force of the Gods, the bodies of those whose haires did smoke, and crash, assume the spirit of a man, and feel, and hear, and walk, and come whither the stink of their haire led them, and insteed of Bæotius the young man, come skipping, and leaping with joy, and love into the house. Austin [Augustine] also reports, that he heard of some women Sorceresses, that were so versed in these kind of arts, that by giving cheese to men, they could presently turn them into working cattell [cattle], and the work being done, restored them into men again.

Chap. xlii. Of the wonderful vertues of some kinds of Sorceries.

Now I will shew you what some of the Sorceries are, that by the example of these there may be a way opened for the consideration of the whole subject of them. Of these therefore the first is menstruous bloud [blood], which, how much power it hath in Sorcery, we will now consider; for, as they say, if it comes over new wine, it makes it soure, and if it doth but touch the Vine it spoyles [spoils] it for ever, and by its very touch it makes all Plants, and Trees barren, and they that be newly set, to die; it burns up all the hearbs [herbs] in the garden, and makes fruit fall off from the Trees, it darkens the brightness of a looking glass, dulls the edges of knives, and razors, dims the beauty of Ivory, and makes Iron presently rusty, it makes brass rust, and smell very strong: it makes dogs mad, if they do but tast [taste] of it, and if they being thus mad shall bite any one, that wound is incurable: it kils [kills] whole hives of Bees, and drives them from the hives that are but touched with it, it makes linnen [linen] black that are boyled [boiled], it makes Mares cast their foal if they do but touch it, and makes women miscarry if they be but smeared with it: it makes Asses barren as long as they eat of the corn that hath been touched with it. The ashes of menstruous clothes, if they be cast upon purple garments that are to be washed, change the colour of them, and takes away colours from flowers.

They say that it drives away tertian, and quartane Agues, if it be put into the wooll of a black Ram, and tyed [tied] up in a silver bracelet, as also if the soles of the patients feet be noynted [anointed] therewith, and especially if it be done by the woman her self, the patients not knowing of it; moreover it cures the fits of the falling sickness. But most especially it cures them that are affraid [afraid] of water, or drink after they are bitten with a mad dog, if onely a menstruous cloth be put under the cup. Besides, they report, that if menstruous women shall walk naked about the standing corn, they make all cankars [cankers], worms, beetles, flyes [flies], and all hurtfull things fall off from the corn: but they must take heed that they do it before Sun rising [sunrise], or else they will make the corn to wither. Also they say that they are able to expell hail, tempests, and lightnings, more of which Pliny makes mention of. Know this, that they are a greater poyson [poison] if they happen in the decrease of the Moon, and yet much greater, if they happen betwixt the decrease, and change of the Moon: But if they happen in the Eclypse [eclipse] of the Moon or Sun, they are an incurable poyson [poison]. But they are of greatest force of all, when they happen in the first years, even in the years of virginity, for if they do but touch the posts of the house there can no mischeif [mischief] take effect in it. Also they say that the threads of any garment touched therewith, cannot be burnt, and if they be cast into the fire, it will spread no further. Also it is said that the root of Peony being given with Castor [oil], and smeared over with a menstruous cloth, cureth the falling sickness. Moreover if the stomack [stomach] of a Hart be burnt or rosted [roasted], and to it be put a perfuming made with a menstruous cloth, it will make crass-bows [cross-bows] useless for the killing of any game: The haires of a menstruous woman put under dung, breed Serpents: and if they be burnt, will drive away Serpents with their smell. So great a poysonous [poisonous] force is in them, that they are poyson [poison] to poysonous [poisonous] creatures. There is also Hippomanes, which amongst Sorceries is not the least taken notice of, and it is a little venemous [venomous] piece of flesh as big as a fig, and black, which is in the forehead of a Colt newly foaled, which unless the Mare her self doth presently eat, she will never after love her foals, or let it suck. And for this cause they say there is a most wonderful power in it to procure love, if it be powdered, and drank in a cup with the blood of him that is in love. There is also another Sorcery, which is called by the same name, viz. Hippomanes, viz. a venemous [venomous] humour, issuing out of the share of a Mare what time she desires a horse, of which Virgill makes mention, when he sings

Hence comes that poison which the Shepherds call Hippomanes, and from Mares groines doth fall, The wofull [woeful] bane of cruell stepdames use, And with a charme 'mongst powerfull drugs infuse.

Of this doth Juvenall the Satyrist [Satirist] make mention.

Hippomanes, poysons [poisons] that boyled [boiled] are, and charmes Are given to Sons in law, with such like harmes.

Apollonius also in his Argonauticks makes mention of the hearb [herb] of Prometheus, which he saith groweth from corrupt blood dropping upon the earth, whilest the Vultur [vulture] was gnawing upon the liver of Prometheus upon the hill Caucasus. The flowre [flower] of this hearb [herb], he saith, is like Saffron, having a double stalk hanging out, one farther then the other the length of a cubit, the root under the earth, as flesh newly cut, sends forth a blackish juice as it were of a beech; with which, saith he, if any one shall after he hath performed his devotion to Proserpina, smear over his body, he cannot be hurt either with sword, or fire. Also Saxo Gramaticus [Grammaticus] writes, that there was a certain man called Froton, who had a garment, which when he had put on he could not be hurt with the point or edge of any weapon. The civet Cat also abounds with Sorceries: for, as Pliny reports, the posts of a dore [door] being touched with her blood, the Arts of Juglers [jugglers] and Sorcerers are so invallid, that the Gods cannot be called up, and will by no means be perswaded to talk with them. Also that they that are anoynted [anointed] with the ashes of the ankle bone of her left foot, being decocted with the blood of a Weesell [weasel] shall become odious to all. The same also is done with the eye, being decocted. Also it is said that the straight gut is administered against the injustice, and corruption of Princes, and great men in power, and for success of Petitions, and to conduce to ending of suits, and controversies, if any one hath never so little of it about him, and that if it be bound unto the left arm, it is such a present [?] charm, that if any man do but look upon a woman, it will make her follow him presently; and that the skin of her [i.e. the civet cat's] forehead doth withstand bewitchings. They say also that the blood of a

Basilisk, which they call the blood of Saturn, hath such great force in Sorcery, that it procures for him that carryes it about him, good success of his Petitions, from great men in power, and of his prayers from God, and also remedies of diseases, and grant of any priveledge [privilege]. They say also that a tyck [tick], if it be pulled out of the left eare of a dog, and if be it altogether black, hath great vertue in the prognostick of life, for if the sick party shall answer him that brought it in, who standing at his feet, & shall ask of him concerning his disease, there is certain hope of life, and that he shall dye [die], if he make no answer. They say also, that a stone that is bit with a mad dog hath power to cause discord, if it be put in drink, and that he shall not be barked at by dogs, that puts the tongue of a dog in his shooe [shoe] under his great toe, especially if the hearb [herb] of the same name, viz. houndstongue be joyned with it. And that a membrane of the secondines of a dog doth the same; and that dogs will shun him that hath a dogs heart. And Pliny reports that there is a red toad that lives in bryers [briars], and brambles, and is full of Sorceries and doth wonderfull things: for the little bone which is in his left side, being cast into cold water, makes it presently very hot, by which also the rage of dogs is restrained, and their love is procured, if it be put in drink; and if it be bound to any one, it stirreth up lust. On the contrary, the litle bone which is on the right side, makes hot water cold, and that it can never be hot again, unless that be taken out, also it is said to cure quartanes if it be bound to the sick in a snakes skin, as also all other feavors [fevers], and restrain love, and lust. And that the spleen, and heart is an effectual remedy against the poisons of the said Toad. Thus much Pliny writes. Also it is said that the sword, with which a man is slain, hath wonderfull power in Sorceries: For if the snaffle of the bridle, or spurs be made of it, they say that with these any horse, though never so wild, may be tamed, and gentled: and that if a Horse should be shod with shooes [shoes] made with it, he would be most swift and fleet, and never, though never so hard rod [rode], tire. But yet they will that some Characters, and names should be written upon it. They say also, if any man shall dip a sword, wherewith men were beheaded, in wine; and the sick drink thereof, he shall be cured of his quartane. They say also that a cup of liquor being made with the brains of a Bear, and drank out of the skull, shall make him that drinks it, to be as fierce, and as raging as a Bear, and think himself to be changed into a Bear, and judge all things he sees to be Bears, and so to continue in that madness, untill the force of that draught shall be dissolved, no other distemper being all the while perceived in him.

Chap. xliii. Of Perfumes, or Suffumigations, their manner, and power.

Some Suffumigations also, or perfumings, that are proper to the Stars, are of great force for the opportune receiving of Celestiall gifts under the rayes of the Stars, in as much as they do strongly work upon the Aire, and breath. For our breath is very much changed by such kind of vapours, if both vapours be of another like: The Aire also being through the said vapours easily moved, or affected with the qualities of inferiours, or those Celestiall, daily, and quickly penetrating our breast, and vitals, doth wonderfully reduce us to the like qualities; Wherefore Suffumigations are wont to be used to [by] them that are about to Sooth-say [soothsay], for to affect their fancy, which indeed being duly appropriated to any certain Deities, do fit us to receive divine inspiration: So they say that fumes made with Lin-seed [linseed], and Flea-bane seed, and roots of Violets, and Parsly [parsley], doth make one to fore-see [foresee] things to come, and doth conduce to prophecying. Let no man wonder how great things suffumigations can do in the Aire, especially when he shall with Porphyrius [Porphyry] consider, that by certain vapours exhaling from proper suffumigations, airy spirits are presently raised, as also Thundrings, and Lightnings, and such like things. As the Liver of a Chamelion [chameleon] being burnt on the top of the house, doth, as it is manifest, raise showers, and Lightnings. In like manner the head, and throat, if they be burnt with Oken [oaken] wood, cause Storms, and

Lightnings. There are also suffumigations under opportune influencies of Stars, that make the images of spirits forthwith appear in the Aire, or elswhere. So they say, that if of Coriander, Smallage, Henbane, and hemlock be made a fume, that spirits will presently come together; hence they are called spirits Hearbs [herbs]. Also it is said that a fume made of the root of the reedy Hearb [herb] Sagapen, with the juice of Hemlock, and Henbane, and the Hearb [herb] Tapsus Barbatus, red Sanders, and black Poppy, makes spirits and strange shapes appear: and if Smallage be added to them, chaseth away spirits from any place, and destroyes their visions. In like manner a fume made of Calamint, Peony, Mints, and Palma Christi, drives away all evil spirits, and vain imaginations. Moreover it is said that by certain fumes certain Animals are gathered together, and put to flight, as Pliny mentions concerning the stone Liparis, that with the fume thereof all beasts are called out; so the bones in the upper part of the throat of a Hart, being burnt, gather all the Serpents together, but the horn of the Hart being burnt doth with its fume chase them all away. The same doth a fume of the feathers of Peacocks. Also the lungs of an Asse being burnt, puts all poisonous things to flight; the fume of the burnt hoof of a Horse drives away Mice, the same doth the hoof of a Mule, with which also if it be the hoof of the left foot, Flies are driven away; And they say, if a house or any place be smoaked [smoked] with the gall of a Cutle fish [cuttle-fish], made into a confection with red Storax, Roses, and Lignum-aloes, and if then there be some Sea Water, or blood cast into that place, the whole house will seem to be full of Water, or blood; and if some Earth of plowed ground be cast there, the Earth will seem to quake. Now such kinds of vapours we must conceive do infect any body, and infuse a vertue into it, which doth continue long, even as any contagious, or poisonous vapour of the Pestilence, being kept for two yeers [years] in the Wall of a house, infect the inhabitants, and as the contagion of Pestilence, or Leprosie [leprosy] lying hid in a garment, doth long after infect him that wears it. Therefore were certain suffumigations used to images, rings, and such like instruments of Magick, and hid treasures, and as Porphyrius [Porphyry] saith, very effectually. So they say, if any one shall hide Gold, or Silver, or any other pretious [precious] thing, the Moon being in conjunction with the Sun, and shall fume the place with Coriander, Saffron, Henbane, Smallage, and black Poppy, of each a like quantity, bruised together, and tempered with the juice of Hemlock, that which is so hid shall never be found, or taken away, and that spirits shall continually keep it: and if any one shall endeavour to take it away, he shall be hurt by them, and shall fall into a frensie [frenzy]. And Hermes saith, that there is nothing like the fume of Sperma Ceti [spermaceti] for the raising of spirits: wherefore if a fume be made of that, and Lignum-aloes, Pepperwort, Musk, Saffron, red Storax tempered together, with the blood of a Lapwing, it will quickly gather airy spirits together, and if it be used about the graves of the dead, it gathers together spirits, and the Ghosts of the dead. So, as often as we direct any work to the Sun, we must make suffumigations with Solary things, if to the Moon, with Lunary things, and so of the rest. And we must know, that as there is a contrariety and enmity in Stars, and spirits, so also in suffumigations unto the same. So there is also a contrariety betwixt Lignum-aloes, and Sulphur, Frankincense, and Quick-silver [quicksilver], and spirits that are raised by the fume of Lignum-aloes, are allayed by the burning of Sulphur. As Proclus gives an example of a spirit, which was wont to appear in the form of a Lion, but by the setting of a Cock before it, vanished away, because there is a contrariety betwixt a Cock, and a Lyon [lion], and so the like consideration, and practise is to be observed concerning such like things.

Chap. xliv. The Composition of some fumes appropriated to the Planets. We make a suffumigation for the Sun in this manner, viz. of Saffron, Amber-gryse [ambergris], Musk, Lignum-aloes, Lignum-balsaim [lignum balsam], the fruit of the Laurell, Cloves, Myrrh, and Frankincense, all which being bruised, and mixt in such a proportion as may make a sweet odour, must be incorporated with the brain of an Eagle, or the blood of a white Cock, after the manner of Pils [pills], or Trochiscks [troches].

For the Moon we make a suffumigation of the head of a Frog dryed [dried], the eyes of a Bull, the seed of white Poppy, Frankincense, and Camphir [camphor], which must be incorporated with Menstruous blood, or the blood of a Goose.

For Saturne take the seed of black Poppy, of Henbane, root of Mandrake, the Load-stone [loadstone], and Myrrh, and make them up with the brain of a Cat, or the blood of a Bat.

For Jupiter take the seed of Ash, Lignum-aloes, Storax, the gum Benjamin [benzoin], the Lazule [lazuli] stone, the tops of the feathers of a Peacock, and incorporate them with the blood of a Stork, or a Swallow, or the brain of a Hart.

For Mars take Euphorbium, Bdellium, gum Armoniack, the roots of both Hellebors [hellebores], the Load stone [loadstone], and a little Sulphur, and incorporate them all with the brain of a Hart, the blood of a Man, and the blood of a black Cat.

For Venus take Musk, Amber-gryse [ambergris], Lignum-aloes, red Roses, and red Corall, and make them up with the brain of Sparrows, and the blood of Pigeons.

For Mercury take Mastick, Frankincense, Cloves, and the Hearb [herb] Cinquefoile, and the stone Achates, and incorporate them all with the brain of a Fox, or Weesel [weasel], and the blood of a Pie [magpie].

Besides, to Saturne are appropriated for fumes all odoriferous roots, as Pepper-wort root, &c. and the Frankincense tree: to Jupiter odoriferous fruits, as Nutmegs, Cloves: to Mars all odoriferous wood, as Sanders [sandalwood], Cypress, Lignum-balsaim [lignum balsam], and Lignum-aloes: to the Sun, all Gums, Frankincense, Mastick, Benjamin, Storax, Laudanum [labdanum, i.e. Cistus], Amber-gryse [ambergris], and Musk; to Venus Flowers, as Roses, Violets, Saffron, and such like: to Mercury all Pils [peels] of Wood and fruit, as Cinnamon, Lignum Cassia, Mace, Citron pill [lemon peel], and Bayber-ries, and whatsoever seeds are odoriferous; to the Moon the leaves of all Vegetables, as the leaf Indum, the leaves of the Myrtle, and Bay-tree. Know also, that according to the opinion of the Magicians, in every good matter, as love, good will, and the like, there must be a good fume, odoriferous, and pretious [precious]; and in every evill matter, as hatred, anger, misery, and the like, there must be a stink-ing fume, that is of no worth. The twelve Signes also of the Zodiack have their proper fumes, as Aries hath Myrrh, Taurus, Pepper-wort [pepperwort], Gemini, Mastick; Cancer, Camphir [camphor], Leo, Frankincense, Virgo Sanders [sandalwood], Libra, Galbanum, Scor-pio, Opoponax, Sagittarius, Lignum-aloes, Capricornus, Benjamin [benzoin], Aquarius, Euphorbium, Pisces, red Storax. But Hermes de-scribes the most powerfull fume to be, viz. that which is compounded of the seven Aromaticks, according to the powers of the seven Plan-ets, for it receives from Saturne, Pepper-wort [pepperwort], from Jupiter, Nutmeg, from Mars, Lignum-aloes, from the Sun, Mastick, from Venus Saffron, from Mercury, Cinnamon, and from the Moon, the Myrtle.

Chap. xlv. Of Collyries, Unctions, Love-Medicines, and their vertues.

Moreover Collyries, and Unguents, conveying the vertues of things Naturall, and Celestiall to our spirit, can multiply, transmute, trans-figure, and transform it accordingly, as also transpose those vertues which are in them into it, that so it cannot act only upon its own body, but also upon that which is neer [near] it, and affect that by visible rayes, charmes, and by touching it, with some like quality. For because our spirit is the subtile, pure lucid, airy, and unctuous vapour of the blood; it is therefore fit to make Collyries of the like vapours, which are more sutable [suitable] to our spirit in subtance, for then by rea-son of their likeness, they do the more stir up, attract, and transform the spirit. The like vertues have certain ointments, and other confections. Hence by the touch sometimes sickness, poisonings, and love is induced; some things, as the hands, or garments being anointed: Also by kisses, some things being held in the mouth, love is induced, as in Virgil we read that Venus prayes Cupid

That when glad Dido hugs him in her lap
At royall feasts, crown'd with the cheering Grape,
When she imbracing [embracing], shall sweet kisses give, Inspire hid Flame, with deadly bane deceive,
He would ----- -----

Now the sight, because it perceives more purely, and cleerly [clearly] then the other senses, and fastening in us the marks of things more acutely, and deeply, doth most of all, and before others agree with the Phantastick spirit, as is apparent in dreams, when things seen do more often present themselves to us then things heard, or any thing coming under the other senses. Therefore when Collyries transform visuall spirits, that spirit doth easily affect the imagination, which indeed being affected with divers species, and forms, transmits the same by the same spirit unto the outward sense of sight, by which occasion there is caused in it a perception of such species, and forms in that manner, as if it were moved by externall objects, that there seem to be seen terrible images, and spirits, and such like: so there are made Collyries, making us forthwith to see the images of spirits in the Aire, or elsewhere, as I know how to make of the gall of a man, and the eyes of a black Cat, and of some other things. The like is made also of the blood of a Lapwing, of a Bat, and of a Goat, and they say, if a smooth shining piece of Steel be smeered [smeared] over with the juice of Mugwort, and made to fume, it will make invocated spirits to be seen in it. So also there are some suffumigations, or unctions, which make men speak in their sleep, to walk, and to do those things which are done by men that are awake, and sometimes to do those things, which men that are awake cannot, or dare not do. Some there are that make us to hear horrid, or delectable sounds, and such like. And this is the cause why Maniacall, and Melancholy men believe they see, and hear those things without, which their imagination doth only fancy within, hence they fear things not to be feared, and fall into wonderfull, and most false suspicions, and fly when none pursueth them, are angry, and contend, no body being present, and fear where no fear is. Such like passions also can magicall confections induce, by Suffumigations, by Collyries, by Unguents, by potions, by poisons, by lamps, and lights, by looking glasses, by images, enchantments, charms, sounds, and Musick. Also by divers rites, observations, ceremonies, religions, and superstitions; all which shall be handled in their places. And not only by these kind of arts, passions, apparitions, and images induced, but also things themselves, which are really changed, and transfigured into divers forms, as the Poet relates of Proteus, Periclimenus, Acheloas, and Merra, the daughter of Erisichthon: So also Circe changed the companions of Ulysses, & of old in the sacrifices of Jupiter Lycæus, the men that tasted of the inwards of the sacrifices, were turned into Wolves, which Pliny saith, befell a certain man called Demarchus, the same opinion was Austin [Augustine] of: for he saith, whilest he was in Italy, he heard of some women that by giving Sorceries in cheese to travellors [travelers], turned them into working Catle [cattle], and when they had done such work as they would have them, turned them into men again, and that this befell a certain Father called Prestantius. The Scriptures themselves testify that Pharao's [pharaoh's] Sorcerers turned their rods into Serpents, and water into blood, and did such like things.

Chapter xlvi. Of naturall alligations, and suspensions.
When the soul of the world, by its vertue doth make all things that are naturally generated, or artificially made, fruitfull, by infusing into them Celestiall properties for the working of some wonderfull effects, then things themselves not only when applyed by suffumigations, or Collyries, or oyntments [ointments], or potions, or any other such like way, but also when they being conveniently wrapt [wrapped] up, are bound to, or hanged about the neck, or in any other way ap-

plyed, although by never so easy a contact, do impress their vertue upon us. By these alligations therefore, suspensions, wrappings up, applications, and contacts the Accidents of the body, and mind are changed into sickness, health, boldness, fear, sadness, and joy, and the like: They render them that carry them, gratious [gracious], or terrible, acceptable, or rejected, honoured, and beloved, or hatefull, and abominable. Now these kind of passions are conceived to be by the abovesaid, infused no otherwise, then is manifest in the graffing [grafting] of trees, where the vitall vertue is sent, and Communicated from the trunk to the twig graffed [grafted] into it, by way of contact and alligation; so in the female Palme tree, when she comes neer to the male, her boughs bend to the male, and are bowed: which the gardeners seeing, bind ropes from the male to the female, which becomes straight again, as if it had by this continuation of the rope received the vertue of the male. In like manner we see, that the cramp-fish being touched afar off with a long pole, doth presently stupify [stupefy] the hand of him that toucheth it. And if any shall touch the sea Hare with his hand or stick, doth presently run out of his wits. Also if the fish called Stella [starfish], as they say, being fastned [fastened] with the blood of a Fox and a brass nail to a gate, evill medicines can do no hurt. Also it is said, that if a woman take a needle, and beray it with dung, and then wrap it up in earth, in which the carkass carcass of a man was buryed [buried], and shall carry it about her in a cloth which was used at the funerall, that no man shall be able to ly [have sex] with her as long as she hath it about her. Now by these examples we see, how by certain alligations of certain things, as also suspensions, or by a simple contact, or the continuation of any thread, we may be able to receive some vertues thereby. It is necessary that we know the certain rule of alligation, and suspension, and the manner which the Art requires, viz. that they be done under a certain, and sutable [suitable] constellation, and that they be done with wyer [wire], or silken threads, with hair, or sinews of certain animals. And things that are to be wrapped up must be done in the leaves of hearbs [herbs], or the skins of animals, or fine cloths, and the like, according to the sutable-ness [suitability] of things: as if you would procure the solary vertue of any thing, this being wrapped up in bay leaves, or the skin of a Lion, hang it about thy neck with a golden thread, or a silken thread of a yallow [yellow] colour, whilest the Sun rules in the heaven: so thou shalt be endued with the Solary vertue of that thing. But if thou dost desire the vertue of any Saturnine thing, thou shalt in like maner take that thing whilest Saturn raignes, and wrap it up in the skin of an Ass, or in a cloth used at a funerall, especially if thou desirest it for sadness, and with a black thread hang it about thy neck. In like man-ner we must conceive of the rest.

Chapter xlvii. Of Rings, and their compositions.

Rings also, which were alwaies much esteemed of by the Ancients, when they are opportunely made, do in like manner impress their vertue upon us, in as much as they do affect the spirit of him that carries them with gladness or sadness, and render him courteous, or terrible, bold, or fearfull, amiable, or hatefull; in as much as they do fortifie us against sickness, poisons, enemies, evill spirits, and all man-ner of hurtfull things, or, at least will not suffer us to be kept under them. Now the manner of making these kinds of Rings, is this, viz. when any Star ascends fortunately, with the fortunate aspect, or con-junction of the Moon, we must take a stone, and Hearb [herb] that is under that Star, and make a Ring of the Metall that is sutable [suit-able] to this Star, and in it fasten the stone, putting the Hearb [herb], or root under it; not omitting the inscriptions of images, names, and Characters, as also the proper suffumigations, but we shall speak more of these in another place, where we shall treat of Images, and Characters. So we read in Philostratus Jarchus, that a wise Prince of the Indians bestowed seven Rings made after this manner, marked with the vertues, and names of the seven Planets, to Apollonius, of which he wore every day one, distinguishing them according to the names of the dayes, by the benefit of which he lived above one hundred and thirty years, as also alwaies retained the beauty of his youth. In like manner Moses the Law-giver, and ruler of the Hebrews, being skilled in the Egyptian Magick, is said by Josephus to have made Rings of love, and oblivion. There was also, as saith Aristotle, amongst the Cireneans a Ring of Battus, which could procure love and honour. We read also that Eudamus a cerain Philosopher made Rings against the bites of Serpents, bewitchings, and evil spirits. The same doth Josephus relate of Solomon. Also we read in Plato that Gygus, King of Lydia had a Ring of wonderfull, and strange vertues, the seal of which, when he turned it toward the palm of his hand, no body could see him, but he could see all things: by the opportunity of which Ring he ravished the Queen, and slew the King his Master, and killed whomsoever he thought stood in his way, and in these villanies no body could see him, and at length by the benefit of this Ring be became King of Lydia.

Chapter xlviii. Of the vertue of places, and what places are sutable to every Star.

There be wonderfull vertues of places accompanying them, either from things there placed, or by the influences of the Stars, or in any other way. For as Pliny relates of a Cuckow [cuckoo], in what place any one doth first hear him, if his right foot be marked about and, and that foot-step [footprint] digged up, there will no Fleas be bred in that place where it is scattered. So they say that the dust of the track of a Snake being gathered up, and scattered amongst Bees, makes them return to their hives. So also that the dust, in which a Mule hath rolled himself, being cast upon the Body, doth mitigate the heat of love, and that the dust wherein a Hawk hath rolled her self, if it be bound to the body in a bright red cloth, cures the quartane. So doth the stone taken out of the nest of a Swallow, as they say, presently relieve those that have the falling sickness [epilepsy], and being bound to the party, continually preserve them, especially if it be rolled in the blood, or heart of a Swallow. And it is reported That if any one shall cut a veine, and being fasting, shall go over a place where any one lately fell with the fit of a Falling sickness [epilepsy], that he shall fall into the same disease. And Pliny reports, that to fasten an Iron naile in that place where he that fell with a fit of the Falling sickness first pitched his head, will free him from his disease. So they say that an Hearb [herb] growing upon the head of any image, being gathered, and bound up in some part of ones garment with a red thread, shall presently allay the headach [headache]; and that any Hearb [herb] gathered out of the brooks or rivers before Sun rising, and no body see him that gathers it, shall cure the Tertian, if it be bound to the left arm, the sick party not knowing what is done.

But amongst places that are appropriated to the Stars, all stinking places, dark, underground, religious, and monrnfull places, as Church-yards, tombes, and houses not inhabited by men, and old, tottering, obscure, dreadfull houses, and solitary dens, caves, and pits, also fish-ponds, standing pools, fennes, and such like are appropriated to Saturne. Unto Jupiter are ascribed all privileged places, Consistories of noble men, Tribunals, Chaires, places for Exercises, Schools, and all beautifull, and clean places, scattered, or sprinkled with divers odours. To Mars, fiery, and bloody places, furnaces, bake-houses, shambles, places of execution, and places where there have been great battailes [battles] fought, and slaughters made, and the like. To the Sun, light places, the Serene Aire, Kings Pallaces [palaces], and Princes Courts, Pulpits, Theators [theaters], Thrones, and all kingly, and Magnificent places. To Venus, pleasant fountains, green Meadows, flowrishing [flourishing] Gardens, garnished beds, stews (and according to Orpheus) the sea, the sea shore, baths, dancing-places, and all places belonging to women. To Mercury, shops, schools, warehouses [warehouses], Exchange for Merchants, and the like. To the Moon, wildernesses, woods, rocks, hils [hills], mountains, forrests [forests], fountains, waters, rivers, seas, sea-shores, ships, groves, high-waies [highways], and granaries for Corn, and such like. Upon this account they that endeavor to procure love, are wont to bury for a certain time the instruments of their art, whether they be rings, images, looking-glasses, or any other, or hide them in a stew house, because in that place they will contract some venerall faculty, no otherwise then things that stand in stinking places, become stinking, and those in an Aromaticall place, become Aromaticall, and of a sweet savour. The four corners of the Earth also pertain to this matter. Hence they that are to gather a Saturnall, Martiall, or Joviall Hearb [herb], must look towards the East, or South, partly because they desire to be orientall from the Sun, and partly, because of their principall houses, viz.> Aquarius, Scorpius [Scorpio],Sagittarius are Southern signes, so also are Capricornus, and Pisces. But they that will gather a Venerall, Mercuriall. or Lunary Hearb [herb], must look towards the West, because they delight to be western, or else they must look Northward, because their principall houses, viz. Taurus, Gemini, Cancer, Virgo are Northern signes, so in any Solary work we must look towards the Eas, or South, but rather towards the Solary body, and light.

Chapter xlix. Of Light, Colours, Candles, and Lamps, and to what Stars, Houses, and Elements severall colours are ascribed.
Light also is a quality that partakes much of form, and is a simple act, and a representation of the understanding: it is first diffused from the Mind of God into all things, but in God the Father, the Father of Light, it is the first true light; then in the Son a beautifull overflowing brightness, and in the Holy Ghost a burning brightness, exceeding all Intelligencies; yea, as Dyonisius saith, of Seraphins, In Angels therefore it is a shining intelligence diffused, an abundant joy beyond all bounds of reason yet received in divers degrees, according to the Nature of the intelligence that receives it; Then it descends into the Celestiall bodies, where it becomes a store of life, and an effectuall propagation, even a visible splendor. In the fire a certain naturall liveliness infused into it by the heavens.
And lastly in men, it is a clear discourse of reason, an knowledge of

divine things, and the whole rationall: but this is manifold, either by reason of the disposition of the body, as the Peripateticks will have it, or which is more true, by reason of the good pleasure of him that bestows it, who gives it to every one as he pleaseth. From thence it passeth to the fancy, yet above the sense, but only imaginable, and thence to the sence [senses], but especially to that of the eyes; In them it becomes a visible clearness, and is extended to other perspicuous bodies, in which it becomes a colour, and a shining beauty, but in dark bodies it is a certain beneficiall and generative vertue, and penetrates, to the very center, where the beames of it being collected into a narrow place, it becomes a dark heat, tormenting, and scorching, so that all things perceive the vigour of the light according to their capacity, all which joyning to it self with an enlivening heat, and passing through all things, doth convey its qualities, and vertues through all things. Therefore Magicians forbid the Urin [urine] of a sick man to be sprinkled in the shadow a sick man, or to be uncovered against the Sun or the Moon, because the rayes of the light penetrating, bringing suddenly with it the noxious qualities of the sick bodies, convey them into the opposite body, and affect that with a quality of the same kind. This is the reason why Enchanters have a care to cover their Enchantments with their shadow. So the Civet cat make all Dogs dumb with the very touch of her shadow. Also there are made artificially some Lights, by Lamps, Torches, Candles, and such like, of some certain thing, and liquors opportunely chosen, according to the rule of the Stars, and composed amongst themselves according to their congruity, which when they be lighted, and shine alone, are wont to produce some wonderfull, and Celestiall effects, which men many times wonder at, as Pliny reports out of Anaxilaus, of a poison of Mares after copulation, which being lighted in Torches, doth monstrously represent a sight of horse heads: the like may be done of Asses, and flies, which being tempered with wax, & lighted, make a strange sight of flies: and the skin of a Serpent lighted in a Lamp, maketh Serpents appear. And they say when Grapes are in their flower, if any one shall bind a Viall to them full of Oile, and shall let it alone till they be ripe, and then the Oile be lighted in a Lamp, it makes Grapes to be seen. And so in other fruits. If Centory be mixed with Honey, and the blood of a Lapwing, and be put in a Lamp, they that stand about will seem a great deal bigger then they are wont: and if it be lighted in a clear night, the Stars will seem to be scattered the one from the other. Such force also is in the inke of the Cuttle fish, that it being put into a Lamp, makes Black-mores [blackamoors] appear. It is also reported, that a Candle made of some certain Saturnine things, if being lighted, it be extinguished in the mouth of a man newly dead, will afterwards, as oft as it shines alone, bring great sadness, and fear upon them that stand about it. Of such like Torches, Lamps, doth Hermes speak more of, also Plato, and Chyrannides, and of the latter writers Albertus in a certain Treatise of this particular thing. Colours also are a kind of lights, which being mixed with things, are wont to expose them to those Stars, to which they are agreeable. And we shall afterwards speak of some colours, which are the lights of the Planets, by which even the natures of fixed Stars themselves are understood, which also may be applyed to the flames of Lamps, and Candles. But in this place we shall relate how the colours of inferiour mixt things are distributed to divers Planets. For all colours, black, lucid, earthy, leaden, brown, have relation to Saturne. Saphire [Sapphire], and airy colours, and those which are alwaies green, clear, purple, darkish, golden, mixed with Silver, belong to Jupiter.

Red colours, and burning, fiery, flaming, violet, purple, bloody, and iron colours, resemble Mars. Golden, Saffron, purple, and bright colours, resemble the Sun. But all white, fair, curious, green, ruddy, betwixt saffron, and purple, resemble Venus, Mercury, and the Moon. Moreover amongst the houses of the heaven [signes of the zodiac], the first and seventh hath white colour: the second, and twelfth green: the third, and eleventh saffron: the fourth, and the tenth red: the fift, and ninth honey colour: the sixt, and eighth, black. The Elements also have their colours, by which Naturall Philosophers judge of the complexion and property of their nature; For an earthy colour, caused of coldness, and dryness is brown, and black, and manifests black Choller [choler], and a Saturnine nature; the blew [blue] tending towards whiteness, doth denote flegme [phlegm]: for cold makes white, moisture and dryness makes black: reddish colour shews blood, but fiery, flaming, burning hot, shew choller [choler], which by reason of its subtilty, and aptness to mix with others, doth cause divers colours more: for if it be mixed with blood, and blood be most predominant, it makes a florid red; if choller [choler] predominate, it makes a redish [reddish] colour; if there be an equall mixtion, it makes a sad red. But if adust choller [choler] be mixed with blood, it makes a Hempen colour, and red, if blood predominate, and somewhat red if choller [choler] prevaile; but if it be mixed with a melancholy humour, it makes a black colour, but with malancholy [melancholy], and flegme [phlegm] together, in an equall proportion, it makes a Hempen colour: If flegme [phlegm] abound, a mud colour, if melancholy, a blewish [bluish]; but if it be mixed with flegme [phlegm] alone, in an equall proportion, it makes a citrine [citron] colour; if unequally, a pale, or palish. Now all colours are more prevalent, when they be in silk, or in metals, or in perspicuous substances, or pretious [precious] stones; and in those things which resemble Celestiall bodies in colour, especially in living things.

Chapter l. Of Fascination, and the Art thereof.

Fascination is a binding, which comes from the spirit of the Witch, through the eyes of him that is bewitched, entering to his heart. Now the instrument of Fascination is the spirit, viz. a certain pure, lucid, subtile vapour, generated of the purer blood, by the heat of the heart. This doth alwaies send forth, through the eyes, rayes like to it self; Those rayes being sent forth, do carry with them a spirituall vapour, and that vapour a blood, as it appears in bleer [bleary], and red eyes, whose raies [rays] being sent forth to the eyes of him that is opposite, and looks upon them, carries the vapour of the corrupt blood, together with it self, by the contagion of which, it doth infect the eyes of the beholder with the like disease. So the eye being opened, and intent upon any one with a strong imagination, doth dart its beams, which are the Vehiculum of the spirit into the eyes of him that is opposite to him, which tender spirit strikes the eyes of him that is bewitched, being stirred up from the heart of him that strikes, and possesseth the breast of him that is stricken, wounds his heart, and infects his spirit. Whence Apuleius saith, Thy eyes sliding down through my eyes, into mine inward breast, stir up a most vehement burning in my Marrow. Know therefore that men are most bewitched, when with often beholding they direct the edge of their sight to the edg [edge] of their sight that bewitch them, and when their eyes are reciprocally intent one upon the other, and when raies [rays] are joyned to raies, and lights to lights, for then the spirit of the one is joyned to the spirit of the other, and fixeth its sparks: So are strong ligations made, and so most vehement loves are inflamed with the only raies of the eyes, even with a certain sudden looking on, as if it were with a dart, or stroke penetrating the whole body, whence then the spirit, and amorous blood being thus wounded, are carried forth upon the lover, and enchanter, no otherwise then the blood, and spirit of the vengeance of him that is slain, are upon him that slayes him. Whence Lucretius sang concerning those amorous bewitchings.

The body smitten is, but yet the mind
Is wounded with the darts of Cupid blind.
 All parts do Simpathize [sympathize] i' th' wound, but know The blood appears in that which had the blow.

So great is the power of Fascination, especially when the vapours of the eyes are subservient to the affection. Therefore Witches use Collyries, ointments, alligations, and such like, to affect, and corroborate the spirit this or that manner. To procure love, they use venereall collyries, as Hippomanes, the blood of Doves, or Sparrows, and such like. To induce fear, they use Martiall Collyries, as of the eyes of

Wolves, the Civet Cat, and the like. To procure misery or sickness, they use Saturnine, and so of the rest.

6

Section 6

Chapter li. Of certain observations, producing wonderfull Vertues.

They say that certain acts, and observations have a certain power of naturall things, that they believe diseases may be expelled, or brought thus, and thus. So they say that quartanes may be driven away if the parings of the nails of the sick be bound to the neck of a live Eel in a linnen clout [linen cloth], and she be let go into the water. And Pliny saith, that the paring of a sick mans nailes of his feet, and hands being mixed with wax, cure the quartan, tertian, and quotidian Ague, and if they be before Sun rising fastened to another mans gate, will cure such like diseases. In like manner let all the parings of the nailes be put into Pismires caves [anthills], and they say that that which begun to draw the nailes first must be taken, and bound to the neck, and by this means will the disease be removed. They say that by Wood stricken with lightning, and cast behind the back with ones hands, any disease may be cured, and in quartanes a piece of a naile from a Gibbet, wrapt up in Wooll, and hanged about the neck, cures them; also a Rope doth the like, that is taken from a Gallows, and hid under ground, that the Sun cannot reach it.

Also the throat of him that hath a hard swelling, or imposthume [aposteme, abscess], being touched with the hand of him that dyed [died] by an immature death, is cured thereby. Also they say, that a woman is presently eased of her hard travel [labor], if any one shall put into the bed, where the woman in travel [labor] is, a stone, or dart, with which either of these Animals, viz. a Man, a Boar, or a Bear were at one blow killed. The same also, as they say, doth a spear that is pulled out of the body of a man, if it shall not first touch the ground; also they say that Arrows pulled out of the body of a man, if they have not touched the Earth, and be put under any one lying down, will procure love; Also they say that the falling sickness is cured by meat made of the flesh of a wild beast, slain in the same manner as a man is slain. Also they say that a mans eyes that are washed three times with the water wherein he hath washed his feet, shall never be sore or bleer [bleary]. It is said that some do cure diseases of the groin with threed [thread] taken out of the Weavers Loom, being tyed [tied] in nine, or seven knots, the name of some Widow being named at every knot. Also the Spleen of Catle [cattle] extended upon pained Spleens, cures them, if he that applies it, saith that he is applying a medicine to the Spleen to cure, and ease it: After this, they say, the patient must be shut into a sleeping room, the dore [door] being sealed up with a Ring, and some verse be repeated over nineteen times. The Urine of a green Lizard cures the same disease, if it be hanged up in a pot before the patients bed-chamber, so that he may, as he comes in and out, touch it with his hand.

Also a Lizard killed in the Urine of a Calf, as they say, retains his lust that put it in: but he that shall put his own Urine into a Dogs Urine, is said to be made thereby dull to venerous acts, and to feel a benummedness in his loins. They say, that if ones own Urine be dropped upon the foot in the morning, it is a remedy against all evil medicines. And a little Frog climbing up a tree, if any one shall spit in his mouth, and then let him escape, is said to cure the Cough. It is a wonderfull thing, but easy to experience, what Pliny speaks of, If any one shall be sorry for any blow that he hath given another afar off, or nigh at hand, if he shall presently spit into the middle of that hand with which he gave the blow, the party that was smitten shall presently be freed from pain. This hath been approved of in a four-footed beast that hath been sorely hurt. Some there are that aggravate the blow before they give it. In like maner spitle [spittle] carried in the hand, or to spit in the shooe [shoe] of the right foot before it be put on, is good when any one passeth through a dangerous place. They say that Wolves will not come to a field, if one of them be taken, and the blood let by little and little out of his legs, being unbroken, with a knife, and sprinkled about the outsides of the field, and he himself be buried in that place, from which he was first drawn. The Methanenses, Citizens of Trezenium, accounted it as a present remedy for preserving of Vines from the wrong of the Southern wind, having alwaies found it by most certain experience; if whilest the wind blows, a white Cock should be pulled to pieces in the middle by two men, both which keeping their part, must walk round the Vineyard, and both meeting in the place from whence they began their Circuit, must that place bury the pieces of the Cock. They say also that if any one shall hold a Viper over a vapour with a staffe, he shall prophecy, and that the staffe wherewith a Snake was beaten is good against diseases of breeding women. These things Pliny recites. It is said also in gathering roots and hearbs [herbs], we must draw three circles round about them, first with a sword, then dig them up, taking heed in the mean time of a contrary wind. Also they say, that if any one shall measure a dead man with a rope, first from the Elbow to the biggest finger, then from the shoulder to the same finger, and afterwards from the head to the feet, making thrice those mensurations, if any one afterward shall be measured with the same rope in the same maner, he shall not prosper, but be unfortunate, and fall into misery, and sadness. And Albertus out of Chyrannis saith, that if any woman hath enchanted thee to love her, take the sheet [gown] she lies in, and piss through her hood, and her right sleeve, out of doors, and the enchantment will be quitted. And Pliny saith, that to sit by women great with child [pregnant], or when a medicine is given to any one of them, the fingers being joyned [joined] together like the teeth of a Kemb [comb], is a charm. This was known by experience in Alcumena breeding Hercules: and so much the worse, if that be done about one, or both knees. Also to sit cross legged, is Sorcery, therefore it was forbiden [forbidden] to be done in the Counsels of Princes, and Rulers, as a thing which hindred all acts. And it is said, if any one standing before the door call the man by his name, that is lying with a woman, and he answer, if then he fasten a knife, or needle on the door, and break it, the edge being downward, he that is in the bed with the woman cannot couple with her as long as those things shall be there.

Chapter lii. Of the Countenance, and Gesture, the Habit, and Figure of the Body, and to what Stars any of these do answer; whence Physiognomy, and Metoposcopy, and Chyromancy [Chiromancy], Arts of divination, have their grounds. The countenance, gesture, the motion, setting, and figure of the body, being accidentall to us, conduce to the receiving of Celestiall gifts, and expose us to the superiour bodies, and produce certain effects in us, no otherwise then in Hellebor, which when thou gatherest, if thou pullest the leaf upward, it draws the humors upward, and causeth vomiting; if downward, it causeth purging, by drawing the humor downward. How much also the countenauce, gesture, do affect the sight, imagination, and Animall spirit, no man is ignorant. So they that couple for generation, for the most part are wont to make an impression on the children that are then begotten, of that countenance which they themselves then form, or imagine: So a mild, and cheerfull countenance of a Prince in the City, makes the people joyfull: but fierce, and sad, terrifies them: so the gesture, and countenance of any one lamenting, doth easily move to pitty [pity]: So the shape of an amiable person, doth easily excite to love. Thou must know that such like gestures, and figures, as harmonies of the body do expose it no otherwise to the Celestials, then odours, and the spirit of a Medicine, and internall passions do the soul. For as Medicines, and passions of the mind are by certain dispositions of the Heaven increased so also the gesture, and motion of the body do get an efficacy by certain influences of the heavens.

For there are gestures resembling Saturne, which are melancholy, and sad, as are beating of the breast, striking of the head: also such as are Religious, as the bowing of the knee, and a fixt look downwards, as of one praying, also weeping, and such like, as are used by an Austere, and Saturnine man, such an one as the Satyrist describes, saying,

With hang'd down head, with eyes fixed to the ground, His raging words bites in, and muttering sound
He doth express with powting [pouting] lips -----

A cheerfull, and honest countenance, a worshipfull gesture, clapping of the hands, as of one rejoycing [rejoicing], and praising; also the bending of the knee, with the head lifted up, as of one that is worshiping, are ascribed to Jupiter. A sowre [sour], fierce, cruell, angry, rough countenance, and gesture, are ascribed to Mars. Solary are honourable, and couragious [courageous] gestures, and countenances: also walkings abroad, bending of the knee, as of one honoring a King with one knee. Venereal, are dances, embraces, laughters, amiable, and cheerfull countenances. Mercuriall are inconstant, quick, variable, and such like gestures, and countenances. Lunary are such as are moveable, poisonfull, and childish, and the like. And as we have spoke of gestures, so also are the shapes of men distinct. For Saturne bespeaks a man to be of a black, and yellowish colour, lean, crooked, of a rough skin, great veines, hairy all over his body, little eyes, of a frowning forehead, of a thin beard, great lips, eyes intent upon the ground, of a heavy gate [gait], striking his feet together as he walks, crafty, witty, a seducer, and murderous. Jupiter signifies a man to be of a pale colour, darkish red, a handsome body, good stature, bold, of great eyes, not black altogether, large pupill, short nostrils, not equall, great teeth before, curld hair, of good disposition, and manners. Mars makes a man red, of a red hair, round face, yellowish eyes, of a terrible, and sharp looks, bold, jocund, proud, crafty. The Sun makes a man of a tauny [tawny] colour, betwixt yellow and black, dasht [dashed] with red, of a short stature, yet of a handsome body, without much hair, and curld, of yellow eyes, wise, faithfull, desirous of praise. Venus signifies a man to be tending towards blackness, but more white, with mixture of red, of a handsome body, a fair, and round face, fair hair, fair eyes, the blackness whereof is more intense, of good manners, and honest love, also kind, patient, and jocund; Mercury signifies a man not much white, or black, of a long face, high forehead, fair eyes, not black, to have a streight [straight], and long nose, thin beard, long fingers, to he ingenious, a subtile inquisitor, turn-coat, and subject to many fortunes. The Moon signifies a man to be in colour white, mixed with a little red, of a fair stature, round face, with some marks in it, eyes not fully black, frowning forehead, also kind, gentle, sociable.

The Signes also, and faces of Signes have their figures, and shapes, which he that would know, must seek them out in books of Astrology. Lastly, upon these figures, and gestures, Physiognomy, and Metoposcopy, arts of divination do depend: Also Chyromancy [chiromancy], foretelling future events, not as causes, but as signes through like effects, caused by the same cause. And although these divers kinds of divinations may seem to be done by inferiour, and weak signes, yet the judgements of them are not to be slighted, or condemned, when prognostication is made by them, not out of superstition, but by reason of the harmoniacall correspondency of all the parts of the body. Whosoever therefore doth the more exactly imitate the Celestiall bodies, either in nature, study, action, motion, gesture, countenance, passions of the mind, and opportunity of the season, is so much the more like to the heavenly bodies, and can receive larger gifts from them.

Chapter liii. Of Divination, and its kinds.

There are some other kinds of divinations, depending upon naturall causes, which are known to every one in his art, and experience, to be in divers things; by which Physitians [physicians], husbandmen, shepheards [shepherds], Mariners, and every one of these out of probable signes do Prognosticate. Many of these kinds Aristotle made mention of in his Book of Times. Amongst which Auguria, and Auspicia are the chiefest, which were in former time in such esteem amongst the Romanes, that they would do nothing that did belong to private or publique [public] business without the counsell of the Augures: Cicero also in his Book of Divinations largely declares, that the people of Tuscia would do nothing without this art. Now there are divers kinds of Auspicia's: for some are called Pedestria (i.e.) which are taken from four-footed beasts: Some are called Auguria, which are taken from birds: Some are Celestiall, which are taken from thundrings, and lightnings; some are called Caduca (i.e.) when any fell in the temple, or elsewhere; Some were sacred, which were taken from sacrifices. Some of these were called Piacula, and sad Auspicia, as when a sacrifice escaped from the Altar, or being smitten made a bellowing, or fell upon another part of his body then he should. To these is added Exauguration, viz., when the rod fell out of the hand of the Augure, with which it was the custome to view, and take notice of the Aupicium. Michael Scotus makes mention of twelve kinds of Auguria's, viz. Six on the right hand, the names of which he saith are Fernova, Fervetus, Confert, Emponenthem, Sonnasarnova, Sonnasarvetus: and the other six on the left hand, the names of which are, Confernova, Confervetus, Viaram, Herrenam, Scassarnova, and Scassarvetus. Then expounding their names, he saith, Fernova is an Augurium; when thou goest out of thy house to do any business, and in going thou seest a man, or a bird going, or flying, so that either of them set himself before thee upon thy left hand, that is a good signification, in reference to thy business. Fervetus is an Augurium; when thou shalt go out of thy house for to do any business, and in going thou findest or seest a bird, or a man resting himself before thee on the left side of thee, that is an ill sign in reference to thy business: Viaram is an Augurium; when a man or a bird in his journey, or flying passeth before thee, coming from the right side of thee, and bending toward the left, goeth out of thy sight, that is a good sign concerning thy business. Confernova is an Augurium; when thou dost first find a man, or a bird going, or flying, and then he rest himself before thee on thy right side, thou seeing of it, that is a good sign concerning thy business; Confervetus is an Augurium; when first thou findest, or seest a man, or a bird bending from thy right side, it is an ill sign concerning thy business. Scimasarnova is an Augurium; when a man, or a bird comes behind thee, and outgoeth thee, but before he comes at thee, he rests, thou seeing of him on thy right side, it is to thee a good sign. Scimasarvetus is an Augurium; when thou seest a man, or bird behind thee, but before he comes to thee he rests in that place, thou seeing of it, is a good sign.

[Confert is an Augurium; when a man or bird in journeying, or flying shall pass behind thee, coming from the left side of thee, and bending toward thy right, pass out of thy sight, and is an evill sign concerning thy business.]

Scassarvetus is when thou seest a man, or a bird passing by thee, and resting in a place on thy left side, it is an evill sign to thee.

[Scassarnova is when thou seest a man, or a bird passing by thee, and resting in a place on thy right side, is an Augurium of good to thee.]

Emponenthem is when a man, or a bird, coming from thy left side, and passing to thy right, goeth out of thy sight without resting, it is a good sign. Hartena is an Augurium; if a man or a bird coming from thy right hand, passing behind thy back to thy left, and thou shall see him resting any where, this is an evill sign. Thus much Scotus. The Ancients did also prognosticate from sneesings [sneezings], of which Homer in the seventeenth book of his Odyssey makes mention, because they thought they proceeded from a sacred place, viz. the head, in which the intellect is vigourous, and operative. Whence also whatsoever speech came into the breast, or mind of a man rising in the morning unawares, is said to be some presage, and an Augurium.

Chapter liiii. Of divers certain Animals, and other things which have a signification in Auguria's [auguries].

All the Auspicia [auspices] which first happen in the beginning of any enterprise are to be taken notice of: as, if in the beginning of thy work thou shalt perceive that Rats have gnawn thy garments, desist from thy undertakings; If going forth thou shalt stumble at the threshold, or if in the way thou shalt dash thy foot against any thing, forbear thy journey; If any ill omen happen in the beginning of thy business, put off thy undertakings, least thy intentions be wholly frustrated, or accomplished to no purpose; but expect and wait for a fortunate hour for the dispatching of thy affairs with a better omen. We see that many Animals are, by a naturall power imbred in them, prophet-icall. Doth not the Cock by his crowing diligently tell you the hours of the night, and morning, and with his wings spread forth chase away the Lion; and many birds with their singing, and chattering, and flies by their sharp pricking foretell rain, and Dolphins by their of-ten leaping above the water, fore-run [forwarn of] tempests. It would be too long to relate all the passages, which the Phrygians, Cilicians, Arabians, Umbrians, Tuscians, and other peoples, which follow the Auguria's, learned by birds. These they have proved by many experi-ments, and examples. For in all things the Oracles of things to come are hid: but those are the chiefest which Ominall [omenal] birds shall foretell. These are those which the Poets relate were turned from men into birds. Therefore what the Daw declares, hearken, and mark, ob-serving her setting as she sits, and her manner of flying, whether on the right hand, or left, whether clamorous, or silent, whether she goes before, or follows after, whether she waits for the approach of him that passeth by, or flies from him, and which way she goes; all these things must be diligently observed. Orus Apollo saith in his Hyero-glyphicks [Hieroglyphics], Daws that are twins signifie marriage, be-cause this Animall brings forth two eggs, out of which male, and female must be brought forth: But if (which seldom happens) two males be generated, or two females, the males will not couple with any other females, nor females with any other males, but will alwaies live without a mate; and solitary. Therefore they that meet a single

Daw, divine thereby that they shall live a single life. The same also doth a black Hen Pigeon betoken; for after the death of her mate, she alwaies lives single. Thou shalt as carefully observe Crows, which are as significant as Daws, yea, and in greater matters. It was Epictetus the Stoicks Philosophers judgment, who was a Sage Author, that if a Crow did croke [croak] over against any one, it did betoken some evill, either to his body, fortune, honour, wife, or children. Then thou shall take heed to Swans, who foreknow the secrets of the waters, for their cheerfulness doth presage happy events not only to Marriners [mariners], but all other travellers, unless they be overcome by the coming over of a stronger [bird], as of an Eagle, who by the most potent Majesty of her soveraignty [sovereignty] makes null the predictions of all other birds, if she speaks to the contrary; for she flies higher then all other birds, and is of more acute sight, and is never excluded from the secrets of Jupiter: She portends advancement, and victory, but by blood; because she drinks no water but blood. An Eagle flying over the Locrensians, fighting against the Crotoniensians gave them victory. An Eagle setting her self unawares upon the Target of Hiero, going forth to the first War, betokened that he should be King. Two Eagles sitting all day upon the house at the birth of Alexander of Macedonia, did portend to him an omen of two Kingdomes, viz. Asia, and Europe. An Eagle also taking off the hat of Lucias Tarquinius Priscus, Son to Demarathus the Corinthian (flying from home by reason of some discord, and being come into Hetraria, and going to Rome) and then flying high with it, and afterwards putting it upon his head again, did portend to him the Kingdome of the Romans. Vulturs [Vultures] signifie difficulty, hardness, ravenousness, which was verified in the beginning of building of Cities. Also they foretell the places of slaughter, coming seven dayes before hand; and because they have most respect to that place where the greatest slaughter shall be, as if they gaped after the greatest number of the slain; therefore the ancient Kings were wont to send out spies to take notice what place the Vulturs [vultures] had most respect to. The Phoenix promiseth singular good success, which being seen anew, Rome was built very auspiciously. The Pellican [pelican], because she hazards her self for her young, signifies that a man should out of the zeal of his love undergo much hardship. The painted bird gave the name to the City of Pictavia, and foreshewed the lenity of that people by its colour, and voice. The Heron is an Augurium of hard things. The Stork is a bird of concord, and makes concord. Cranes gives us notice of the trechery [treachery] of enemies. The bird Cacupha betokens gratitude, for she alone doth express love to her Dam [mother], being spent with old age. On the contrary, Hippopotamus that kils [kills] his Dam [mother], doth betoken ingratitude for good turn, also injustice. The bird Origis is most envious, and betokens envy.

Amongst the smaller birds, the Pie is talkative, and foretels [foretells] guests. The bird Albanellus flying by any one, if from the left to the right, betokens cheerfulness of entertainment, if contrarywise, betokens the contrary. The scritch [screech] Owl is alwaies unlucky, so also is the horn Owl, who because she goes to her young by night unawares, as death comes unawares, is therefore said to foretell death: yet sometimes, because she is not blind in the dark of the night, doth betoken diligence, and watchfulness, which she made good, when she sate upon the spear of Hiero. Dido, when she sees the unlucky Owl, pittied [pitied] Æneas, whence the Poet sang,

The Owl sitting on top of th' house alone,
Sends forth her sad complaints with mournfull tone.

And in another place,

The slothfull Owl by mortals is esteem'd A fatall omen -----

The same same bird sang in the Capitoll when the Romane affaires were low at Numantia, and when Fregelia was pulled down for a conspiracy made against the Romans. Almadel saith, that Owls, and night-ravens, when they turn aside to strange countries, or houses, betoken the death of the men of that country, and those houses; for those birds are delighted with dead Carkases [carcasses], and perceive them before hand. For men that are dying have a neer affinity with dead Carkases [carcasses]. The Hawk also is a foreteller of contention, as Naso sings.

We hate the Hawk, because that arms amongst She alwaies lives

-----

Lelius the Embassadour of Pompey was slain in Spain amongst the Purveyours, which misfortune, a Hawk flying over the head, is said to foretell. And Almadel saith, that these kind of birds fighting amongst themselves, signifie the change of a Kingdome; but if birds of another kind shall fight with them, and are never seen to come together again, it portends a new condition, and state of that Country. Also little birds by their coming to, or departing from, foreshew that a family shall be inlarged [enlarged], or lessened, and their flight, by how much the more serene it is, by so much the more laudable. Whence Melampus the Augure conjectured at the slaughter of the Greeks by the flight of little birds, when he saith, Thou seest that no bird taketh his flight in fair weather. Swallows, because when they are dying they provide a place of safety for their young, do portend a great patrimony, or Legacy after the death of friends. A Bat meeting any one running away, signifies an evasion: for although she have no wings, yet she flies. A Sparrow is a bad omen to one that runs away, for she flies from the Hawk, and makes hast [haste] to the Owl, where she is in as great danger: yet in love she is fortunate, for being stirred up with lust, couples seven times in an hour. Bees are a good omen to Kings, for they signifie an obsequious people. Flies signifie importunity, and impudency, because being oftentimes driven away, they do yet continually return. Also domestick birds are not without some Auguria's, for Cocks by their crowing promote hope, and the journey of him that is undertaking it. Moreover Livia the mother of Tiberius, when she was great with him, took a Hen-Egg and hatched it in her bosome, and at length came forth a Cock chick with a great comb, which the Augures interpreted that the child that should be born of her should be King. And Cicero writes that at Thebais Cocks, by their crowing all night, did presage that the Bætians would obtain victory against

the Lacedæmonians: and the reason is according to the Augures inter-
pretations, because that bird when he is beaten is silent, but when he
himself hath overcome, crows. In like manner also omens of events
are taken from beasts. For the meeting of a Weesel [weasel] is ominous, also meeting of a Hare is an ill omen to a traveller, unless she
be taken. A Mule also is bad, because barren. A Hog is pernicious, for
such is his nature, and therefore signifies pernicious men. A Horse betokens quarrellings, and fightings: whence Anchises seeing of white
Horses, cries out in Virgil,

With War are Horses arm'd, yea threaten War.

But when they are joyned together in a Chariot, because they draw
with an equall yoke, they signifie that peace is to be hoped for. An
Asse is an unprofitable creature, yet did Marius good, who when
he was pronounced an enemy to his country, saw an Asse disdain-
ing provender that was offered to him, and running to the water, by
which Augury, he supposing he saw a way of safety shewed to him,
intreated the aid of his friends, that they would convey him to the
Sea; which being granted, he was set into a little ship, and so escaped the threats of Silla the Conqueror. If the Foal of an Asse meet
any one going to an Augury, he signifies labor, patience, and hinderances. A Wolf meeting any one is a good sign, the effect whereof was
seen in Hiero of Sicilia, from whom a Wolf snatching away a book
whilest he was at school, confirmed to him the success of the Kingdom: but yet the Wolf makes him speechless whom he sees first. A
Wolf rent in pieces a Watchman of P. Africanus, and C. Fulvius at
Minturn, when the Romane Army was overcome by the fugitives in
Sicilia. Also he signifies perfidious men, such as you can give no credit
to: which was known in the progeny of Romanes. For the faith which
they long since sucked from their mother the Wolf, and kept to themselves from the beginning, as by a certain law of nature, passed over
to their posterity. To meet a Lion, seeing she is amongst Animals
the strongest, and striking terrour into all the rest, is good. But for a
woman to meet a Lionesse, is bad, because she hinders conception, for

a Lionesse brings forth but once. To meet Sheep, and Goats is good. It is read also in the Ostentarian of the Tuscians, if this Animall shall wear any unusuall colour, it portends to the Emperour plenty of all things, together with much happiness. Whence Virgil to Pollio sings thus,

But in the Meadows Rams shall Skarlet [scarlet] bear, And changing, sometimes golden Fleeces wear.

It is good also to meet Oxen treading out Corn, but better to meet them plowing, which although breaking the way hinder thy journey, yet by the favour of their Auspicium will recompence thee again. A Dog in a journey is fortunate, because Cyrus being cast into the woods was nourished by a Dog till he came to the Kingdom, which also the Angel, companion of Tobit did not scorn as a companion. The Castor, because he bites off his Testicles, and leaves them to the Hunters, is an ill omen, and portends that a man will injure himself. Also amongst small Animals, Mice signifie danger. For the same day that they did gnaw Gold in the Capitoll, both the Consuls were intercepted by Hannibal by way of ambush neer Tarentum. The Locust making a stand in any place, or burning the place, hinders one from their wishes, and is an ill omen; on the contrary the Grass- hoppers [grasshoppers] promote a journey, and foretell a good event of things. The Spider weaving a line downwards, is said to signifie hope of money to come. Also the Pismires [ants], because they know how to provide for themselves, and to prepare safe nests for themselves, portend security, and riches, a great Army. Hence, when the Pismires [ants] had devoured a tame Dragon of Tiberius Caesar, it was advised, that he should take heed of the tumult of a multitude. If a Snake meet thee, take heed of an ill tongued enemy; For this Animall hath no power but in his mouth. A Snake creeping into Tiberius his pallace [palace], portended his fall. Two Snakes were found in the bed of Sempronius Gracchus, wherefore a Soothsayer told him, if he would let the male, or the female escape, either he or his wife would shortly dye [die]; he preferring the life of his wife, killed the male, and let the female escape, and within a few dayes he dyed [died]. So a Viper signifies lewd women, and wicked children; and an Eel signifies a man displeased with every body: For she lives apart from all other fishes, nor is ever found in the company of any. But amongst all Auspicia's [auguries] and omens, there is none more effectuall, and potent then man, none that doth signifie the truth more cleerly. Thou shalt therefore diligently note, and observe the condition of the man that meeteth thee, his age, profession, station, gesture, motion, exercise, complexion, habit, name, words, speech, and all such like things. For seeing there are in all other Animals so many discoveries of presages, without all question these are more efficacious, and cleer, which are infused into mans soul; which Tully [Cicero] himself testifies, saying, that there is a certain Auspicium naturally in mens souls of their eternity, for the knowing of all the courses, and causes of things. In the foundation of the City of Rome the head of a man was found with his whole face, which did presage the greatness of the Empire, and gave the name to the Mountain of the Capitoll. The Brutian souldiers [soldiers] fighting against Octavius, and M. Antonius, found an Aethiopian [Ethiopian] in the gate of their Castle; whom though they did slay as a presage of ill success, yet they were unfortunate in the batle [battle], and Brutus, and Cassius both Generals, were slain. Meeting of Monks is commonly accounted an ill omen, and so much the rather, if it be early in the morning, because these kind of men live for the most by the sudden death of men, as Vulturs [vultures] do by slaughters.

Chapter lv. How Auspica's are verified by the light of Naturall instinct, and of some rules of finding of it out.

Auspicia, and Auguria, which foretell things to come by Animals, & birds, Orpheus the divine himself (as we read) did teach and shew first of all, which afterwards were had in great esteem with all Nations. Now they are verified by the light of naturall instinct, as if from this, some lights of divination may descend upon four-footed beasts, winged, and other Animals, by which they are able to presage to us of the events of things: which Virgil seems to be sensible of, when he sings,

Nor think I Heaven on them such knowledge states, Nor that their prudence is above the fates.

Now this Instinct of nature, as saith William of Paris, is more sublime then all humane apprehension, and very neer, and most like to prophecy. By this instinct there is a certain wonderfull light of divination in some Animals naturally, as it manifestly appears in some Dogs, who know by this instinct theeves [thieves], and men, and finde them out, and apprehend them, falling upon them with a full mouth. By the like instinct Vulturs [vultures] foresee future slaughters in batles [battles], and gather together into places where they shall be, as if they fore-saw the flesh of dead Carkases [carcasses]. By the same instinct Partridges [partridges] know their Dam, whichm they never saw and leave the Partridge which stole away her Dams Eggs, & sate upon them. By the same instinct also certain hurtful and terrible things are perceived (the soul of the men being altogether ignorant of them) whence terror, and horror ceaseth much upon men when they think nothing of these things. So a thief lying hid in any house, although no body knows, or thinks of his being there, strikes fear, and terror, and a troublesomeness of mind into the inhabitants of that house, although haply not of all, because the brightness of this instinct is not in all men; yet of some of them. So a harlot being hid in some very large house, is sometimes perceived to be there by some one that is altogether ignorant of her being there. It is mentioned in Histories that Heraiscus a certain Egyptian, a man of a divine nature, could discern unclean women, not only by his eyes, but by their voice, being heard afar off, and thereupon did fall into a most grievous headach [headache]. William of Paris also makes mention of a certain woman in his time, that by the same instinct perceived a man whom she loved, coming two miles off. Also he relates that in his time was a certain Stork convicted of unchastity by the smell of the male, who being judged guilty by a multitude of Storks whom the male gathered together, discovering to them the fault of his mate, was, her feathers being pulled off, torn in pieces by them. He also makes mention of a certain horse, who not knowing his dam [mother], and leaping of [copulating with] her, when afterwards he understood what he had done, bit off his own Stones [testicles] by way of revenge upon himself for his incest. The same doth Varro, Aristotle, and Pliny relate concerning horses. And Pliny makes mention of a certain Serpent, called the Asp, that did such a like thing, for she coming to a certain mans table in Egypt, was there daily fed, and she having brought forth some young, by one of which a son of her hosts was killed, after she knew of it, killed that young one, and would never return to that house any more. Now by these examples you see, how the lights of presage may descend upon some Animals, as signs, or marks of things, & are set in their gesture, motion, voice, flying, going, meat, colour, and such like. For according to the doctrine of the Platonists, there is a certain power put into inferiour things, by which for the most part they agree with the superiours; whence also the tacid consents of Animals seem to agree with divine bodies, and their bodies and affections to be affected with their powers, by the name of which they are ascribed to the Dieties [Deities]. We must consider therefore what Animals are Saturnall, what are Joviall, and what Martiall, and so of the rest, and according to their properties to draw forth their presages: so those birds which resemble Saturn, and Mars, are all of them called terrible, and deadly, as the Scritch [screech] Owl, the Hawlet, and others which we have mentioned before, also the horn Owl, because she is a Saturnall Solitary bird, also nightly, and is reputed to be most unfortunately ominous, of which the Poet saith,

The ugly Owl, which no bird well resents,
Fortels [foretells] misfortunes, and most sad events.

But the Swan is a delicious bird, Venereall, and Dedicated to Phoebus, and is said to be most happy in her presages, especially in the Auspicia's of Mariners, because she is never drowned in water, whence Ovid sings,

Most happy is the cheerfull, singing Swan In her presages -----
----- -----

There are also some birds that presage with their mouth, and singing, as the Crow, Pie, Daw, whence Virgil,

- This did fore-show

Oft from the hollow holm that ominous Crow.

Now the birds that portend future things by their flying are, viz. Buzzards, the bone- Breakers, Eagles, Vulturs [vultures], Cranes, Swans, and the like: for they are to be considered in their flying, whether they fly slowly, or swiftly, whether to the right hand, or to the left, how many fly together: upon this account if Cranes fly apace, they signifie a tempest: when slowly, fair weather. Also when two Eagles fly together, they are said to portend evill, because that is a number of confusion. In like manner thou shalt enquire into the reason of the rest, as this is shewed of number. Moreover it belongs to an artist to observe a similitude in these conjectures, as in Virgil, Venus dissembling, teacheth her son Aeneas in these verses.

- All this is not for naught,

Else we in vain my parents Augury taught, Lo! twice six Swans in a glad company

Joves bird pursued through the etheriall Skie [sky] In Heavens broad tracks: now earth in a long train They seem to take, or taken to disdain;

As they return with sounding wings, they sport, And Heaven surrounding in a long consort.

Just so, I say, thy friends and fleet have gain'd The port, or with full sailes the Bay obtain'd.

Most wonderful is that kind of Auguring of theirs, who hear, & understand the speeches of Animals, in which as amongst the Ancients, Melampus, and Tiresias, and Thales, and Apollonius the Tyanean [Apollonius of Tyana], who as we read, excelled, and whom they report had excellent skill in the language of birds: of whom Philostratus, and Porphyrius [Porphyry] speak, saying, that of old when Apollonius sate in company amongst his friends, seeing Sparrows sitting upon a tree, and one Sparrow coming from elsewhere unto them, making a great chattering and noise, and then flying away, all the rest following him, he said to his companions, that that Sparrow told the rest that an Asse being burdened with wheat fell down in a hole neer the City, and that the wheat was scattered upon the ground: many being much moved with these words, went to see, and so it was, as Apollonius said, at which they much wondered. Also Porphyrius [Porphyry] the Platonist in his third book of Sacrifices, saith, that there was a Swallow: for it was certain, because every voice of any Animall is significative of some passion of its soul, as joy, sadness, or anger, or the like, which voices it is not so wonderfull a thing should be understood by men conversant about them. But Democritus himself declared this art, as saith Pliny, by naming the birds, of whose blood mixed together was produced a Serpent, of which whosoever did eat, should understand the voices of birds. And Hermes saith, if any one shall go forth to catch birds on a certain day of the Kalends of November, and shall boil the first bird which he catcheth, with the heart of a Fox, that all that shall eat of this bird, shall understand the voices of birds, and all other Animals. Also the Arabians say, that they can understand the meaning of bruits [brutes], who shall eat the heart, and liver of Dragons. Proclus also the Platonist believed, and wrote, that the heart of a Mole conduceth to presages. There were also divinations, and Auspicia's which were taken from the inwards of sacrifices, the inventor whereof was Tages, of whom Lucan sang,

And if the Inwards have no credit gained, And if this Art by Tages was but feigned.

The Romane Religion thought that the liver was the head of the inwards. Hence the Sooth-sayers [soothsayers] enquiring after future things in the inwards, did first look into the liver, in which were two heads, whereof the one was called the head for the City, the other for the enemy; and the heads of this, or another part being compared together, they pronounced Victory, as we read in Lucan, that the inwards did signifie the slaughter of Pompeys men, and the Victory of Caesars, according to these verses,

I' th' inwards all defects are ominous

On part, and branch of th' entrals [entrails] doth increase, Another part is weak, and flagging lies,

Beats, and moves with quick pulse the arteries.

Then the bowels being finished, they search the heart. Now if there were a sacrifice found without an heart, or a head was wanting in the Liver, these were deadly presages, and were called piacularia. Also if a sacrifice fled from the Altar, or being smitten, made a lowing, or fell upon any part of his body then he ought to do, it was the like ominous. We read that when Julius Caesar on a day went forth to procession with his purple Robe, and sitting in a golden chair, and sacrificing, there was twice a Heart wanting; And when C. Marius Utica was sacrificing, there was wanting a Liver. Also when Caius the prince, and M. Marcellus, C. Claudius, and L. Petellius Coss: were offering sacrifices, that the Liver was consumed away suddenly: and not long after, one of them dyed [died] of a disease, another was slain by men of Lyguria, the entrals [entrails] foretelling so much: which was thought to be done by the power of the Gods, or help of the divell [devil]: Hence it was accounted a thing of great concernment amongst the Ancients as oft as any thing unusuall was found in the inwards: as when Sylla was sacrificing at Laurentum, the figure of a Crown appeared in the head of the Liver: which Posthumius the Soothsayer interpreted to portend a Victory with a Kingdome, and therefore advised that Sylla should eat those entrals [entrails] himself. The colour also of the inwards is to be considered. Of these Lucan made mention.

Struck at the colour Prophets were with fear,

For with foul spots pale entrals [entrails] tinged were. Both black, and blew [blue], with specks of sprinkled blood They were

There was in times past such a venerable esteem of these arts, that the most potent, and wise men sought after them, yea the Senate, and Kings did nothing without the Counsell of the Augures. But all these in these dayes, partly by the negligence of men, and partly by the authority of the Fathers, are abolished.

Chapter lvi. Of the Sooth sayings of Flashes, and Lightenings, and how Monstrous, and prodigious things are to be interpreted.
Now the Sooth-sayings of Flashes, and Lightenings, and of wonders, and how monstrous, and prodigious things are to be interpreted, the Prophets, and Priests of Hetruscus have taught the Art. For they have ordained sixteen Regions of the Heavens, and have ascribed Gods to every one of them; and besides eleven kinds of Lightenings, and nine Gods, which should dart them forth, by shewing rules for understanding the signification of them. But as often as Monstrous, prodigious, and wondrous things happen, they do presage, as is most certain, some great matter. Now their interpreter must be some excellent conjecturer of similitudes, as also some curious searcher, and of them who at that time are employed about the affairs of Princes, and Provinces. For the Celestials take such care only for Princes, peoples, and provinces, that before the rest they might be prefigured, and admonished, by Stars, by Constellations, by wonders, and by prodigies. Now if the same thing, or the like hath been seen in former Ages, we must consider that very thing, and what happened after that, and according to these, to fortell the same, or the like, because the same signs are for the same things, and the like for like. So prodigies have come before the birth, and death of many eminent men and Kings; as Cicero makes mention of Midas a boy, into whose mouth, whilest he was sleeping, the Pismire [ant] put corns of Wheat, which was an omen of great riches. So Bees sate upon the mouth of Plato when he was sleeping in the Cradle, by which was foretold the sweetness of his speech. Hecuba, when she was bringing forth Paris, saw a burning Torch, which should set on fire Troy, and all Asia. There appeared unto the mother of Phalaris the image of Mercury pouring forth blood upon the earth, with which the whole house was overflowed. The mother of Dionysius dreamed she brought forth a Satyr,

which prodigious dreams the event that followed made good. The wife of Tarquinius Priscus seeing a flame lick the head of Servius Tullius, foretold that he should have the Kingdom. In like manner after Troy was taken, Aeneas disputing with Anchises his father concerning a flight [?], there appeared a flame licking the Crown of Ascanius his head, and doing of him no hurt: which thing, seeing it did portend the Kingdom to Ascanius, perswaded him to depart, for monstrous prodigies did fore-run great and eminent destruction. So we read in Pliny, that M. Attilius, and C. Portius being Consuls, it rained Milk, and Blood, which did presage that a very great Pestilence should the next yeer [year] over-spread Rome.

Also in Lucania it rained spongious [spongeous] Iron, & in the yeer before Marcus Crassus was slain in Parthia; with which also all the souldiers [soldiers] of Lucania, being a very numerous Army, were slain. Also L. Paulus, and C. Marcellus being Consuls, it rained Wool about the Castle of Corisanum, neer which place a yeer [year] after T. Annius was slain by Milus. And in the wars of Denmark, the noise of Arms, and sound of a Trumpet was heard in the Aire. And Livie [Livy] concerning the Macedonian wars, saith, in the yeer when Annibil [Annibal] dyed [died] it rained blood for two dayes. Also concerning the second punick war, he saith, that water mixed with blood came down from Heaven like rain, at that time when Annibal did spoil Italy. A little before the destruction of Leuctra the Lacedemonians heard a noise of Arms in the temple of Hercules, and at the same time in the temple of Hercules the doors that were shut with bars, opened themselves, and the arms that were hanged on the wall, were found on the ground. The like events may be prognosticated of other like things, as oftentimes in times past something hath been foretold of them. But concerning these also, the judgements of the Celestial influencies must not be neglected, of which we shall more largely treat in the following Chapters.

Chapter lvii. Of Geomancy, Hydromancy, Aeromancy, Pyromancy, four Divinations of Elements.

Moreover the Elements themselves teach us fatall events; whence those four famous kinds of Divinations, Geomancy, Hydromancy, Aeromancy, and Pyromancy, have got their names, of which the Sorceress in Lucan seems to boast her self, when she saith,

The Earth, the Aire, the Chaos, and the Skie,
The Seas, the Fields, the Rocks, and Mountains high Foretell the truth

-----

The first therefore is Geomancy, whicb foresheweth future things by the motions of the earth, as also the noise, the swelling, the trembling, the chops, the pits, and exhalation, and other impressions, the art of which Almadel the Arabian sets forth. But there is another kind of Geomancy, which Divines by points written upon the earth, by a certain power in the fall of it, which is not of present speculation; but of that we shall speak hereafter.

Now Hydromancy doth perform its presages by the impressions of water, their ebbing and flowing, their increases, and depressions, their tempests, and colours, and the like; to which also are added visions, which are made in the waters. A kind of Divination found by the Persians, as Varro reports, a boy saw in the water the effigies of Mercury, which foretold in an hundred and fifty verses all the events of Mithridates his War. We read also that Numa Pompilius practiced Hydromancy; for in the water he called up the gods, and learned of them things to come. Which art also Pythagoras, a long time after Numa practised. There was of old a kind of Hydromancy, had in great esteem amongst the Assyrians, and it was called Lecanomancy, from a skin full of water, upon which they put plates of Gold, and Silver, and pretious [precious] Stones, written upon with certain images, names, and characters. To this may be referred that art, by which Lead, and Wax being melted, and cast into the water, do express manifest marks of images, what we desire to know. There were also in former years Fountains that did foretell things to come, as the Fathers-Fountain at

Achaia, and that which was called the water of Juno in Epidaurus; but of these more in the following Chapters, where we shall speak of Oracles.

Hither also may be referred the divination of Fishes, of which kind there was use made by the Lycians in a certain place, which was called Dina, neer the Sea, in a Wood dedicated to Apollo, made hollow in the dry sand, into which, he that went to consult of future things, let down roasted meat, and presently that place was filled with waters, and a great multitude of Fish, and of strange shapes, unknown to men, did appear, by the forms of which the Prophet foretold what should come to pass. These things doth Atheneus more at large relate out of Polycharmus, in the History of the Lycians.

After the same maner doth Aeromancy divine by airy impressions, by the blowing of the Winds, by Rainbows, by Circles about the Moon and Stars, by Mists, and Clouds, and by imaginations in Clouds, and visions in the Aire.

So also Pyromancy divines by fiery impressions, and by Stars with long Tailes, by fiery Colours, by visions, and imaginations in the fire. So the wife of Cicero foretold that he would be Consul the next year, because when a certain man after the Sacrifice was ended, would look in the ashes, there suddenly broke forth a flame. Of this kind are those that Pliny speaks of, that terrene, pale, and buzzing fires presage tempests, Circles about the snuffs of Candles betoken rain; if the flame fly turning, and winding, it portends wind.

Also Torches when they strike the fire before them, and are not kindled. Also when a Coal sticks to Pots taken off from the fire, and when the fire casts off the ashes, and sparkles, or when ashes are hard grown together on the hearth, and when a Coal is very bright.

To these is added Capnomancy, so called from smoak [smoke], because it searcheth into the flame, and smoak [smoke], and thin colours, sounds, and motions, when they are carryed upright, or on one side, or round, which we read in these Verses in Statius.

Let Piety be bound, and on th' Altar laid, Let us implore the Gods for divine aid.

She makes acute, red, towring flames, and bright, Increas'd by th' aire, the middle being white;

And then she makes the flames without all bound, For to wind in and out, and to run round

Like to a Serpent -----

Also in the Aethnean Caves, and Fields of the Nymphs in Apollonia, Auguries were taken from fires, and flames; joyful, if they did receive what was cast into them, and sad, if they did reject them. But of these things we shall speak in the following Chapters, amongst the answers of the Oracles.

Chapter lviii. Of the reviving of the dead, and of sleeping, and wanting victuals many years together.

The Arabian Philosophers agree, that some men may elevate themselves above the powers of their body, and above their sensitive powers; and those being surmounted, receive into themselves by the perfection of the Heavens, and Intelligencies, a divine vigour. Seeing therefore all the souls of men are perpetuall, and also all the spirits obey the perfect souls; Magicians think that perfect men may by the powers of their soul repair their dying bodies with other inferiour souls newly separated, and inspire them again; As a Weesell [weasel] that is killed, is made alive again by the breath, and cry of his Dam [mother]; And Lions make alive their dead Whelps by breathing upon them. And because, as they say, all like things being applyed to their like, are made of the same natures; and every patient, and thing that receives into it self the act of any agent, is endowed with the nature of that agent, and made con-naturall. Hence they think, that to this vivification, or making alive, some Hearbs [herbs], and Magicall confections, such as they say are made of the ashes of the Phoenix, and the cast skin of a Snake do much conduce, which indeed to many seems fabulous, and to some impossible, unless it could be accounted approved by an Historicall faith. For we read of some that have been drowned in water, others cast into the fire, and put upon the fire, others slain in war, others otherwise tryed, and after a few dayes were alive again, as Pliny testifies of Aviola, a man pertaining to the Consull, of L. Lamia, Cæius, Tubero, Corfidius, Gabienus, and many others. Also we read that Aesop the Tale-maker, Tindoreus, Hercules, and Palicy, the sons of Jupiter, and Thalia being dead, were raised to life again; also that many were by Physitians [physicians], and Magicians raised from death again, as the Historians relate of Aesculapius; and we have above mentioned out of Juba, and Xanthus, and Philostratus concerning Tillo, and a certain Arabian, and Apollonius the Tyanean. Also we read that Glaucus, a certain man that was dead, whom they say, beyond all expectation, the Physitians [physicians] coming to see it, the hearb [herb] Dragon-wort restored to life. Some say that he revived by the puting into his body a medicine made of Honey, whence the proverb, Glaucus was raised from death by taking in Honey into his body. Apuleius also relating the manner of these kinds of restorings to life, saith of Zachla the Egyptian prophet: The prophet being thus favourable, layes a certain Hearb [herb] upon the mouth of the body of a young man being dead, and another upon his brest [breast], then turning towards the East, or rising of the propitious Sun, praying silently (a great assembly of people striving to see it) in the first place heaved up his brest [breast], then makes a beating in his veines [CPR!?], then his body to be filled with breath [mouth- to-mouth?], after which the Carkase ariseth, and the young man speaks. If these things are true, the dying souls must, sometimes lying hid in their bodies, be oppressed with vehement extasies [ecstasies], and be freed from all bodily action: So that the life, sense, motion, forsake the body, and so, that the man is not yet truly dead, but lies astonied [dazed], and as it were dead for a certain time. And this is often found, that in times of Pestilence many that are carried for dead to the graves to be buryed [buried], revive again. The same also hath often befeln women, by reason of fits of the Mother. And Rabbi Moises out of the book of Galen, which Patriarcha translated, makes mention of a man, who was suffocated for six dayes, and did neither eat nor drink, and his arteries became hard. And it is said in the same book, that a certain man by being filled with Water, lost the pulse of his whole body, so that the heart was not perceived to move, and he lay like a dead man. Also it is said that a man by reason of a fal [fall] from a high place, or great noise, or long staying under the Water, may fall into a swoun [swoon], which may continue fourty eight [forty-eight] hours, and so lye as if he were dead, his face being very green. And in the same place there is mention made of a man that buried a man that seemed to be dead seventy two hours after his seeming decease, and so killed him, because he buried him alive, and there are given signs whereby it may be known who are alive; although they seem to be dead, and indeed will dye [die], unless there be some means used to recover them, as Phlebotomy, or some other cure. And these are such as very seldom happen. This is the manner, by which we understand Magicians, and Physitians [physicians] do raise dead men to life, as they that were tryed by the stinging of Serpents, were by the Nation of the Marsi, and the Psilli restored to life. Now we may conceive that such kind of extasies [ecstasies] may continue a long time, although a man be not truly dead, as it is in Dor-mice [dormice], and Crocodiles, and many other Serpents, which sleep all Winter, and are in such a dead sleep, that they can scarce be awakened with fire. And I have often seen a Dormouse dissected, and continue immovable, as if she were dead, untill she was boyled [boiled], and when presently in boyling [boiling] the water the dissected members did shew life. Also, although it be hard to be believed, we read in some approved Historians, that some men have slept for many yeers together, and in the time of sleep, untill they awaked, there was no alteration in them, as to make them seem older: The same doth Pliny testifie of a certain boy, whom he saith, being wearied with heat, and his journey, slept fifty seven yeers in a Cave. We read also that Epimenides Gnosius slept fifty seven yeers in a Cave. Hence the proverb arose, To outsleep Epimenides. M. Damascenus tels, that in his time a certain country man being wearied in Germany, slept for the space of a whole Autumn, and the Winter following, under a heap of hay, untill the Summer, when the hay began to be eaten up, then he was found awakened as a man halfe dead, and out of his wits. Eclesiasticall [Ecclesiastical] Histories confirm this opinion concerning the seven sleepers, whom they say slept 196 yeers. There was in Norvegia a Cave in a high Sea shore, where, as Paulus Diaconus, and Methodius the Martyr write, seven men lay sleeping a long time without corruption, and the people that went in to disturb them were contracted, or drawn together, so that after a while, being forewarned by that punishment, they durst not hurt them. Now Xenocrates, a man of no mean repute amongst Philosophers was of opinion, that this long sleeping was appointed by God as a punishment for some certain sins. But Marcus Damascenus proves it by many reasons to be possible, and naturall, neither doth he think it irrationall, that some should without meat, and drink, and avoyding excrements, without consuming, or corruption, sleep many moneths. And this may befall a man by reason of some poisonous potion, or sleepy disease, or such like causes, for certain dayes, moneths, or years, according to the intention, or remission of the power of the medicine, or of the passions of their mind. And Physitians [physicians] say that there are some Antidotes, of which they that take too great a potion, shall be able to endure hunger a long time, as Elias in former time being fed with a certain food by an Angell, walked, and fasted in the strength of that meat, fourty [forty] dayes. And John Bocatius makes mention of a man in his time, in Venice, who would every yeer fast four dayes without any meat. But that was a greater wonder, that there was a woman in lower Germany at the same time, who took no food till the thirteenth yeer of her age, which to us may seem incredible, but that he lately confirmed it; as also he tels of a Miracle of our Age, that his brother Nicolaus Stone, an Helvetian by Nation, who lived twenty yeers in the wilderness without meat, till he dyed [died]. That also is wonderfull which Theophrastus mentions concerning a certain man, called Philinus, who used no meat, or drink, besides Milk. And there are grave Authors who describe a certain hearb [herb] of Sparta, with which they say the Scythians can endure twelve dayes hunger, without meat or drink, if they do but tast [taste] it, or hold it in their mouth.

Chapter lix. Of Divination by Dreams.

There is also a certain kind of Divination by Dreams, confirmed by the traditions of Philosophers, the authorities of Divines, the examples of Histories, and daily experience. A Dreams I call here, not vain Dreams, or idle imaginations: for those are vain, and have no Divination in them, but arise from the remains of watchings, and disturbance of the body. For as the mind is taken up about, and wearied with cares, it suggests it self to him that is asleep. I call that a Dream here, which is caused by the Celestiall influences in the phantastick spirit, mind, or body, being all well disposed. The rule of interpreting this is found amongst Astrologers, in that part which is wrote concerning questions; but yet that is not sufficient, because these kind of Dreams come by use to divers men after a divers manner, and according to the divers quality, and dispositions of the phantastick spirit: wherefore there cannot be given one common rule to all for the interpretation of Dreams. But according to the opinion of Synesius, seeing there are the same accidents to things, and like befall like; so be which hath often fallen upon the same visible thing, hath assigned to himself the same opinion, passion, fortune, action, event, and as Aristotle saith, the memory is confirmed by sence [sense], and by keeping in memory the same thing knowledge is obtained, as also by the knowledge of many experiences, by little, & little, arts, and sciences are obtained. After the same account you must conceive of Dreams. Whence Synesius commands that every one should observe his Dreams, and their events, and such like rules, viz. to commit to memory all things that are seen, and accidents that befall, as well in sleep, as in watching, and with a diligent observation consider with himself the rules by which these are to be examined, for by this means shall a Diviner be able by little, and little to interpret his Dreams, if so be nothing slip out of his memory. Now Dreams are more efficacious, when the Moon over-runs that Sign, which was in the ninth number of tbe Nativity, or revolution of that yeer, or in the ninth Sign from the Sign of perfection. For it is a most true, and certain divination, neither doth it proceed from nature or humane Arts, but from purified minds, by divine inspiration.

We shall now discuss, and examine that which belongs to prophecyings, and oracles.

Chapter lx. Of Madness, and Divinations which are made when men are awake, and of the power of a Melancholy humor, by which Spirits are sometimes induced into mens bodies.

It happens also sometimes, that not only they that are asleep, but also they that are watchfull do with a kind of instigation of minde, Divine, which Divination Aristotle cals ravishment, or a kind of madness, and teacheth that it proceeds from a melancholy humor, saying in his Treatise of divination: Melancholy men, by reason of their earnestness, do far better conjecture, and quickly conceive a habit, and most easily receive an impression of the Celestials. And in his Problemes saith, that the Sibyls, and the Bacchides, and Niceratus the Syracusan, and Amon, were by their naturall Melancholy complexion Prophets, and Poets. The cause therefore of this madness, if it be any thing within the body, is a melancholy humor, not that which they call black choller [choler], which is so obstinate, and terrible a thing, that the violence of it is said by Physitians [physicians], and Naturall Phylosophers [philosophers], besides madness, which it doth induce, also to entice evill spirits to seize upon mens bodies. Therefore we understand a melancholy humor here, to be a naturall, and white choller [choler]. For this, when it is stirred up, burns, and stirs up a madness conducing to knowledge, and divination, especially if it be helped by any Celestiall influx, especially of Saturn, who seeing he is cold, and dry, as is a melancholy humor, hath his influence upon it, increaseth, and preserveth it. Besides, seeing he is the Author of secret contemplation, and estranged from all publike [public] affairs, and the highest of all the planets, doth alwaies as with call his mind from outward businesses, so also makes it ascend higher, and bestows upon him the knowledge, and passages of future things. And this is Aristotles meaning in his book of Problemes. By Melancholy, saith he, some men are made as it were divine, foretelling things to come, and some men are made Poets. He saith also, that all men that were excellent in any Science, were for the most part melancholy. Democritus, and Plato attest the same, saying, that there were some melancholy men, that had such excellent wits, that they were thought, and seemed to be more divine then humane. So also there have been many melancholy men at first rude, ignorant, and untractable, as they say Hesiod, Ion, Tynnichus, Calcinenses, Homer, and Lucretius were, who on a suddain were taken with a madness, and became Poets, and prophecied wonderfull, and divine things, which they themselves scarce understood. Whence divine Plato in Ion saith, many Prophets, after the violence of their madness was abated, do not well understand what they wrote, yet treated acurately [accurately] of each Art in their madness, as all Artists by reading of them judge. So great also they say the power of melancholy is of, that by its force, Celestiall spirits also are sometimes drawn into mens bodies, by whose presence, and instinct, antiquity testifies men have been made drunk, and spake most wonderful things. And that they think happens under a threefold [three-fold] difference, according to a threefold apprehension of the soul, viz. imaginative, rationall, and mentall. They say therefore, when the mind is forced with a melancholy humor, nothing moderating the power of the body, and passing beyond the bonds of the members, is wholly carried into imagination, and doth suddenly become a seat for inferior spirits, by whom it oftentimes receives wonderfull wayes, and forms of manuall Arts. So we see that any most ignorant man doth presently become an excellent painter, or contrivers of building, and to become a master in any such Art. But when these kinds of spirits portend to us future things, they shew those things which belong to the disturbing of the Elements, and changes of times, as rain, tempests, innundations, earthquakes, great mortality, famine, slaughter, and the like. As we read in Aulus Gelius, that Cornelius Patarus his Priest did at the time, when Cesar, and Pompey were to fight in Thessalia, being taken with a madness, foretell the time, order, and issue of the battell [battle]. But when the mind is turned wholly into reason, it becomes a receptacle for midle [middle] spirits. Hence it obtains the knowledge, and understanding of natural, and humane things. So we see that a man sometimes doth on a suddain become a Philosopher, Physitian [physician], or an excellent Orator, and foretels [foretells] mutations of Kingdomes, and restitutions of Ages, and such things as belong to them, as the Sybill [Sibyl] did to the Romanes; but when the mind is wholly elevated into the understanding, then it becomes a receptacle of sublime spirits, and learns of them the secrets of divine things, such as the Law of God, the orders of Angels, and such things as belong to the knowledge of things eternall, and salvation of souls. It foresees things which are appointed by Gods speciall predestination, as future prodigies, or miracles, the prophet to come, and the changing of the law. So the Sybills [Sibyls] Prophecyed of Christ a long time before his coming. So Virgil understanding that Christ was at hand, and remembring what the Sybill [Sibyl] Cumaea had said, sang thus to Pollio.

Last times are come, Cumæa's prophesie
Now from high heaven springs a new progenie, And times great order now again is born,
The Maid returns, Saturnian Realms return.

And a little after intimating that originall sin shall be of no effect, saith,

If any prints of our old vice remain'd
By thee they'r voyd, and fear shall leave the Land; He a Gods life shall take, with Gods shall see Mixt Heroes, and himself their object be,
Rule with paternall power th' appeased earth He shall ----------

Then he adds, that thence the fall of the Serpent, and the poison of the tree of death, or of the knowledge of good, and evill shall be nulled, saying,

The Serpent shall

And the deceitfull hearb [herb] of venome fall.

Yet he intimates that some sparks of originall sin shall remain, when he saith,

Some steps of ancient fraud shall yet be found.

And at last with a most great hyperbole cryes out to his child, as the off-spring [offspring] of God, adoring him in these words,

Dear race of Gods, great stock of Jupiter,

Behold! the world shakes on its ponderous axe,

See earth, and heavens immense, and th' Ocean tracts, How all things at th' approaching Age rejoyce!

Oh! that my life would last so long, and voyce, As would suffice thy actions to rehearse.

There are also some prognosticks, which are in the middle [middle], betwixt naturall, and supernaturall divination, as in those who are neer to death, and being weakened with old Age, do sometimes foresee things to come, because as saith Plato, by how much the more men are less hindred by their sence, so much the more acurately they understand, and because they are neerer to the place whither they must go, and their bonds being as it were a little loosed, seeing they are no more subject to the body, easily perceive the light of divine revelation.

7

Section 7

Chapter lxi. Of the forming of Man, of the external Senses, and also the Inward, and the Mind: of the threefold appetite of the Soul, and passions of the Will.

It is the opinion of some Divines, That God did not immediately creat [create] the body of man, but by the assistance of the heavenly Spirits compound, and frame him; which opinion Alchinous, and Plato favor; thinking that God is the chief Creator of the whole world, of spirits both good and bad, and therefore immortalized them: but that all kinds of mortall animals were made at the command of God; for if he should have created them, they must have been immortall. The spirits therefore mixing Earth, Fire, Aire, and Water together, made of them all, put together, one body, which they subjected to the service of the soul, assigning in it severall Provinces to each power thereof, to the meaner of them, mean and low places: as to Anger the Midriff, to Lust the Womb, but to the more noble senses the Head, as the Tower of the whole body, and then the manifold Organs of Speech. They divide the Sense into External, and Internall. The externall are divided into five, known to every one, to which there are allotted five Organs, or subjects, as it were Foundations; being so ordered, that they which are placed in the more eminent part of the body, have a greater degree of purity. For the Eyes placed in the uppermost place, are the most pure, and have an affinity with the Nature of Fire, and Light: then the Ears have the second order of place, and

purity, and are compared to the Aire: the Nostrils have the third order, and have a middle nature betwixt the Aire, and the Water; then
the Organ of tasting, which is grosser and most like to the nature of
Water: Last of all, the touching is diffused through the whole body,
and is compared to the grossness of Earth. The more pure senses are
those which perceive their Objects farthest off, as Seeing, and Hearing, then the Smelling, then the Tast [taste], which doth not perceive
but those that are nigh. But the touch perceives both wayes, for it perceives bodies nigh; and as Sight discerns by the medium of the Aire,
so the touch perceives by the medium of a stick or pole, bodies Hard,
Soft, and Moist. Now the touch only is common to all animals. For it
is most certain that man hath this sense, and in this, and tast [taste]
he excels all other animals, but in the other three he is excelled by
some animals, as by a Dog, who Hears, Sees, and Smels [smells] more
acutely then Man, and the Linx [lynx], and Eagles see more acutely
then all other Animals, & Man. Now the interior senses are, according to Averrois, divided into four, whereof the first is called Common
sence [sense], because it doth first collect, and perfect all the representations which are drawn in by the outward senses. The second is the
imaginative power, whose office is, seeing it represents nothing, to
retain those representations which are received by the former senses,
and to present them to the third faculty of inward sense, which is the
phantasie, or power of judging, whose work is also to perceive, and
judge by the representations received, what or what kind of thing that
is of which the representations are, and to commit those things which
are thus discerned, and adjudged, to the memory to be kept. For the
vertues thereof in generall, are discourse, dispositions, persecutions,
and flights, and stirrings up to action: but in particular, the understanding of intellectuals, vertues, the manner of Discipline, Counsel,
Election. And this is that which shews us future things by dreams:
whence the Fancy is sometimes named the Phantasticall Intellect. For
it is the last impression of the understanding; which, as saith Iamblicus, is belonging to all the powers of the mind, and forms all fig-

ures, resemblances of species, and operations, and things seen, and sends forth the impressions of other powers unto others: And those things which appear by sence [sense], it stirs up into an opinion, but those things which appear by the Intellect, in the second place it offers to opinion, but of it self it receives images from all, and by its property, doth properly assign them, according to their assimilation, forms all the actions of the soul, and accommodates the externall to the internall, and impresses the body with its impression. Now these senses have their Organs in the head, for the Common sence [sense], and imagination take up the two former Cels [cells] of the brain, although Aristotle placeth the Organ of the Common sence [sense] in the heart, but the cogitative power possesseth the highest, and middle part of the head; and lastly, the memory the hinmost part thereof. Moreover, the Organs of Voice, and Speech are many, as the inward muscles of the breast betwixt the ribs, the breasts, the lungs, the arteries, the windpipe, the bowing of the Tongue, and all those parts and muscles that serve for breathing. But the proper Organ of Speech is the Mouth, in which are framed words, and speeches, the Tongue, the Teeth, the Lips, the Palate, &c. Above the sensible soul, which expresseth its powers by the Organs of the body, the incorporeall mind possesseth the highest place, and it hath a double nature, the one, which inquireth into the causes, properties, and progress of those things which are contained in the order of nature, and is content in the contemplation of the truth, which is therefore called the contemplative intellect. The other is a power of the mind, which discerning by consulting what things are to be done, and what things to be shunned, is wholly taken up in consultation, and action, and is therefore ealled the Active Intellect. This Order of powers therefore nature ordained in man, that by the externall sences [senses] we might know corporeall things, by the internall the representations of bodies, as also things abstracted by the mind and intellect, which are neither bodies, nor any thing like them. And according to this threefold order of the powers of the soul, there are three appetites in the soul: The first is naturall, which is an inclination of nature into its end, as of a stone downward, which is in all stones: another is animal, which the sense follows, and it is divided into irascible, and concupiscible: the third is intellective, which is called the will, differing from the sensitive, in this, the sensitive is of it self, of those things, which may be presented to the senses, desiring, nothing unless in some manner comprehended. But the will, although it be of it self, of all things that are possible, yet because it is free by its essence, it may be also of things that are impossible, as it was in the Devil, desiring himself to be equall with God, and therefore is altered and depraved with pleasure and continuall anguish, whilest it assents to the inferiour powers. Whence from its depraved appetite there arise four passions in it, with which in like manner the body is affected sometimes. Whereof the first is called Oblectation, which is a certain quietness or assentation of the mind or will, because it obeys, and not willingly consents to that pleasantness which the senses hold forth; which is therefore defined to be an inclination of the mind to an effeminate pleasure. The second is called effusion, which is a remission of, or dissolution of the power, viz. when beyond the oblectation the whole power of the mind, and intention of the present good is melted, and diffuseth it self to enjoy it. The third is vaunting, and loftiness, thinking it self to have attained to some great good, in the enjoyment of which it prides it self and glorieth. The fourth and the last is Envy, or a certain kind of pleasure or delight at another mans harm, without any advantage to it self. It is said to be without any advantage to it self, because if any one should for his own profit rejoyce at an other mans harm, this would be rather out of love to himself, then out of ill wil [will] to another. And these four passions arising from a depraved appetite for pleasure, the grief or perplexity it self doth also beget so many contrary passions, as Horror, Sadness, Fear, and Sorrow at anothers good, without his own hurt, which we call Envy, i.e. Sadness at anothers prosperity, as pity is a certain kind of sadness at anothers misery.

Chapter lxii. Of the Passions of the Mind, their Original [origin], difference, and kinds.

The passions of the mind are nothing else but certain motions or inclinations proceeding from the apprehension of any thing, as of good or evill, convenient or inconvenient. Now these kind of apprehensions are of three sorts, viz., Sensual, Rationall, and Intellectuall. And according to these three, are three sorts of passions in the Soul; For when they follow the sensitive apprehension, then they respect a temporall good or evill, under the notion of profitable, or unprofitable, delightfull and offensive, and are called naturall, or animall passions. When they follow the rational apprehension, and so respect good or bad, under the notions of Vertue or Vice, praise or disgrace, profitable or unprofitable, honest or dishonest, they are called rationall, or voluntary passions. When they follow the Intellectuall apprehension, and respect good or bad, under the notion of just or unjust, true or false, they are called intellectuall passions, or synderesis. Now the subject of the passions of the soul, is the concupitive power of the soul, and is divided into concupiscible, and irascible, and both respect good and bad, but under a different notion. For when the concupiscible power respects good, and evil absolutely; Love or Lust, or on the contrary, hatred is caused: When it respects good, as absent, so desire is caused; or evill, as absent, or at hand, and so is caused horror, flying from, or loathing: or if it respect good, as present, then there is caused delight, mirth, or pleasure; but if evill, as present, then sadness, anxiety, grief. But the irascible power respects good or bad, under the notion of some difficulty; to obtain the one, or avoid the other, and this sometimes with confidence: and so there is caused Hope or Boldness; but when with diffidency, then Despair, and Fear. But when that irascible power riseth into revenge, and this be onely about some evill past, as it were of injury or hurt offered, there is caused Anger. And so we find eleven passions in the mind, which are, Love, Hatred, Desire, Horror, Joy, Grief, Hope, Despair, Boldness, Fear, and Anger.

Chapter lxiii. How the passions of the mind change the proper body, by changing the Accidents, and moving the spirit.

The Phantasie, or imaginative power hath a ruling power over the passions of the soul, when they follow the sensuall apprehension. For this doth of its own power, according to the diversity of the Passions, First of all change the proper body with a sensible transmutation, by changing the Accidents in the body, and by moving the spirit upward or downward, inward, or outward, and by producing divers qualities in the members. So in joy, the spirits are driven outward, in fear, drawn back, in bashfulness, are moved to the brain. So in joy, the heart is dilated outward, by little and little, in sadness, is constringed by little, and little inward. After the same manner in anger or fear, but suddenly. Again anger, or desire of revenge produceth heat, redness, a bitter tast [taste], and a looseness.

Fear induceth cold, trembling of the heart, speechlessness, and paleness. Sadness causeth sweat, and a blewish [bluish] whiteness. Pitty [pity], which is a kind of sadness, doth often ill affect the body of him that takes pitty [pity], that it seems to be the body of another man affected. Also it is manifest, that amongst some lovers there is such a strong tye [tie] of love, that what the one suffers, the other suffers. Anxiety induceth dryness, and blackness. And how great heats love stirs up in the Liver, and pulse, Physitians [physicians] know, discerning by that kind of judgement the name of her that is beloved, in an Heroick Passion. So Naustratus knew that Antiochus was taken with the love of Stratonica. It is also manifest that such like Passions, when they are most vehement, may cause death. And this is manifest to all men, that with too much joy, sadness, love, hatred, men many times dye [die], and are sometimes freed from a disease. So we read, that Sophocles, and Dionysius the Sicilian Tyrant, did both suddenly dye [die] at the news of a Tragicall victory. So a certain woman seeing her son returning from the Canensian battle, dyed [died] suddenly. Now what sadness can do, is known to all. We know that Dogs oftentimes dye [die] with sadness for the death of their masters. Sometimes also by reason of these like Passions, long diseases follow, and are sometimes cured. So also some men looking from an high place, by reason of great fear, tremble, are dim-sighted, and weakened, and sometimes loose their senses. So fears, and falling-sickness, sometimes follow sobbing. Sometimes wonderfull effects are produced, as in the son of Cræsus, whom his mother brought forth dumb, yet a vehement fear, and ardent affection made him speak, which naturally he could never do. So with a suddain fall oftentimes life, sense, or motion on a suddain leave the members, and presently again are sometimes returned. And how much vehement anger, joyned with great audacity, can do, Alexander the great shews, who being circumvented with a battle in India, was seen to send forth from himself lightening [lightning] and fire. The Father of Theodoricus is said to have sent forth out of his body, sparks of fire; so that sparkling flames did leap out with a noyse [noise]. And such like things sometimes appear in beasts, as in Tiberius his horse, which is said to send forth a flame out of his mouth.

Chapter lxiv. How the Passions of the mind change the body by way of imitation from some resemblance; Also of the transforming, and translating of men, and what force the imaginative power hath not only over the body, but the soul.
The foresaid Passions sometimes alter the body by way of imitation, the reason of the vertue which the likeness of the thing hath to change it, which power the vehement imagination moves, as in setting the teeth on edge at the sight or hearing of something, or because we see or imagine another to eat sharp or soure things; So he which sees another gape [yawn], gapes also; and some when they hear any one name soure things, their tongues waxeth tart. Also the seeing of any filthy thing causeth nauseousness. Many at the sight of mans blood fall into a swoun [swoon]. Some when they see bitter meat given to any, perceive a bitter spitle [spittle] in their mouth. And William of Paris saith, that he saw a man, that at the sight of a medicine, went to stool

as oft as he pleased; when as neither the substance of the medicine, nor the odour, nor the tast [taste] of it came to him: but only a kind of resemblance was apprehended by him. Upon this account some that are in a dream think they burn, and are in a fire, and are fearfully tormented, as if they did truly burn, when as the substance of the fire is not neer them, but only a resemblance apprehended by their imagination. And sometimes mens bodies are transformed, and transfigured, and also transported, and this oft-times when they are in a dream, and sometimes when they are awake. So Cyprus after he was chosen King of Italy, did very much wonder at, and meditate upon the sight [fight?], and victory of Buls [bulls], and in the thought thereof did sleep a whole night, but in the morning was found horned, no otherwise then by the vegetative power being stirred up by a vehement imagination, elevating corniferous humors into his head, and producing horns. For a vehement cogitation, whilest it vehemently moves the species, pictures out the figure of the thing thought on, which they represent in their blood, and the blood impresseth from it self, on the members that are nourished by it, as upon those of the same body, so upon those of anothers. As the imagination of a woman with child impresseth the mark of the thing longed for upon her infant, and the imagination of a man bit with a mad Dog, impresseth upon his Urine the image of Dogs. So men may grow grey on a suddain. And some by the dream of one night, have grown up from boies [boys] into perfect men. Hitherto may be referred those many scarrs of King Dagobertus, and Marks of Franciscus, which they received, the one whilest he was afraid of correction, the other whilest he did wonderfully meditate upon the wounds of Christ. So, many are transported from place to place, passing over rivers, fires and unpassable places, viz. when the species of any vehement desire, or fear, or boldness are impressed upon their spirits, and, being mixed with vapors, do move the Organ of the touch in their original, together with phantasie, which is the original of locall motion. Whence they stir up the members, and Organs of motion to motion, and are moved without any mistake unto the imagined place, not out of sight, but from the interiour fantasy [phantasy]. So great a power is there of the soul upon the body, that which way soever that imagines, and dreams that it goes, thither doth it lead the body. We read many other examples by which the power of the soul upon the body is wonderfully explained, as is that which Avicen describes of a certain man, who when he pleased could affect his body with the palsie [palsy]. They report of Gallus Vibius, that he did fall into madness, not casually, but on purpose: for whilest he did imitate mad men, he assimilated their madness to himself, and became mad indeed. And Austin [Augustine] makes mention of some men who would move their ears at their pleasure, and some that would move the crown of their head to their forehead, and could draw it back again when they pleased: and of another that could sweat at his pleasure. And it is well known, that some can weep at their pleasure, and pour forth abundance of tears: and that there are some that can bring up what they have swallowed, when they please, as out of a bag, by degrees. And we see that in these dayes there are many who can so imitate, and express the voices of Birds, Cattle, Dogs, and some men, that they can scarce at all be discerned. Also Pliny relates by divers examples, that women have been turned into men. Pontanus testifieth, that in his time, a certain woman called Caietava, and another called Aemilia, who after many years, after they were married, were changed into men. Now how much imagination can do upon the soul, no man is ignorant: for it is neerer to the substance of the soul then the sense is; wherefore it acts more upon the soul then the sense doth. So women by certain strong imaginations, dreams, and suggestions brought in by certain Magicall Arts do oftentimes bind them into a strong loving of any one. So they say that Medea only by a dream, burnt in love towards Jason. So the soul sometimes is by a vehement imagination, or speculation altogether abstracted from the body, as Celsus relates of a certain Presbyter, who as oft as he pleased, could make himself senseless, and lie like a dead man, that when any one pricked, or burnt him, he felt no pain, but lay without any motion or breathing, yet he could, as he said, hear mens voices as it were afar off, if they cryed out aloud. But of these abstractions we shall discourse more fully in the following Chapters.

Chapter lxv. How the Passions of the Mind can work out of themselves upon anothers Body.

The Passions of the Soul which follow the phantasie, when they are most vehement, cannot only change their own body, but also can transcend so, as to work upon another body, so that some wonderfull impressions are thence produced in Elements, and extrinsecall things, and also can so take away, or bring some disease of the mind or body. For the Passions of the Soul are the chiefest cause of the temperament of its proper body. So the Soul being strongly elevated, and inflamed with a strong imagination, sends forth health or sickness, not only in its proper body, but also in other bodies. So Avicen is of the opinion, that a Camell may fall by the imagination of any one. So he which is bitten with a mad Dog presently fals into a madness, and there appear in his Urine the shapes of Dogs. So the longing of a woman with Child, doth act upon anothers body, when it Signs the infant in the womb with the mark of the thing longed for. So, many monstrous generations proceed from monstrous imaginations of women with Child, as Marcus Damascenus reports that at Petra Sancta, a Town scituated [situated] upon the territories of Pisa, viz. a wench that was presented to Charls [Charles] King of Bohemia, who was rough and hairy all over her body, like a wild beast, whom her mother affected with a religious kind of horrour [horror] upon the picture of John Baptist, which was by her bed, in time of conception, afterwards brought forth after this fashion. And this we see is not only in men, but also is done amongst bruit [brute] Creatures. So we read that Jacob the Patriarch, with his speckled Rods set in the watering places, did discolour the Sheep of Laban. So the imaginative powers of Pea-Cocks, and other Birds, whilest they be coupling, impress a colour upon their wings. Whence we produce white Pea-Cocks [peacocks], by hanging round the places where they couple, with white Clothes. Now by these examples it appears how the affection of the phantasie, when it vehemently intends it self, doth not only affect its own proper body, but also anothers. So also the desire of Witches to hurt, doth bewitch men most perniciously with stedfast [steadfast] lookes. To these things Avicen, Aristotle, Algazel, and Gallen assent. For it is manifest that a body may most easily be affected with the vapour of anothers diseased body, which we plainly see in the Plague, and Leprosie [leprosy]. Again, in the vapours of the eyes there is so great a power, that they can bewitch and infect any that are near them, as the Cockatrice, or Basilisk, killing men with their looks. And certain women in Scythia, amongst the Illyrians, and Triballi, killed whomsoever they looked angry upon. Therefore let no man wonder that the body, and soul of one may in like manner be affected with the mind of another, seeing the mind is far more powerfull, strong, fervent, and more prevalent in its motion then vapours exhaling out of bodies; neither are there wanting Mediums, by which it should work, neither is anothers body less subjected to anothers mind, then to anothers body. Upon this account they say, that a man by him affection, and habit only, may act upon another. Therefore Philosophers advise, that the society of evil, and mischievous men must be shunned, for their soul being full of noxious rayes, infects them that are near with a hurtfull Contagion. On the contrary, they advise that the society of good, and fortunate men be endeavored after, because by their nearness they do us much good. For as the smell of Assa-fetida [asafetida], or Musk, so of bad something of bad, of good something of good, is derived upon them that are nigh, and sometimes continues a long time. Now then if the foresaid Passions have so great a power in the Phantasie, they have certainly a greater power in the reason, in as much as the reason is more excellent then the Phantasie; and lastly, they have much greater power in the mind; for this, when it is fixt upon God for any good with its whole intention, doth oftentimes affect anothers body as well as its own with some divine gift. By this means we read that many miracles were done by Apollonius, Pythagoras, Empedocles, Philolaus, and many Prophets, and holy men of our Religion.

But of these more fully in the following Chapters, where we shall discourse of Religion.

Chapter lxvi. That the Passions of the mind are helped by a Celestiall season, and how necessary the Constancy of the mind is in every work. The Passions of the mind are much helped, and are helpfull, and become most powerfull by vertue of the Heaven, as they agree with the heaven, either by any naturall agreement, or by voluntary Election. For, as saith Ptolomeus [Ptolemy], he which chooseth that which is the better, seems to differ nothing from him who hath this of nature. It conduceth therefore very much for the receiving of the benefit of the Heavens, in any work, if we shall by the Heaven make our selves sutable [suitable] to it in our thoughts, affections, imaginations, elections, deliberations, contemplations, and the like. For such like passions do vehemently stir up our spirit to their likeness, and suddenly expose us, and ours to the superior significators of such like passions; and also by reason of their dignity, and neerness to the superiors, do much more partake of the Celestials, then any materiall things. For our mind can through imaginations, or reason by a kind of imitation, be so conformed to any Star, as suddenly to be filled with the vertues of that Star, as if it were a proper receptacle of the influence thereof. Now the contemplating mind, as it withdraws it self from all sense, imagination, nature, and deliberation, and cals [calls] it self back to things separated, unless it exposeth it self to Saturn, is not of present consideration, or enquiry. For our mind doth effect divers things by faith, which is a firm adhesion, a fixt intention, and a vehement application of the worker, or receiver, to him that co-operates in any thing, and gives power to the work which we intend to do. So that there is made as it were in us the image of the vertue to be received, and the thing to be done in us, or by us. We must therefore in every work, and application of things, affect vehemently, imagine, hope, and believe strongly, for that will be a great help. And it is verified amongst Physitians [physicians], that a strong belief, and an undoubted hope, and love towards the Physitian [physician], and medicine, conduce much to health, yea more sometimes than the medicine it self. For the same that the efficacy, and vertue of the medicine works, the same doth the strong imagination of the Physitian [physician] work, being able to change the qualities in the body of the sick, especially when the patient placeth much confidence in the Physitian [physician], by that means disposing himself for the receiving of the vertue of the Physitian [physician], and Physick [=medicine].

Therefore he that works in Magick, must be of a constant belief, be credulous, and not at all doubt of obtaining the effect. For as a firm, and strong belief doth work wonderfull things, although it be in false works, so distrust and doubting doth dissipate, and break the vertu [vertue] of the mind of the worker, which is the medium betwixt both extreams, whence it happens, that he is frustrated of the desired influence of the superiors, which could not be joyned, and united to our labours without a firm, and solid vertue of our mind.

Chapter lxvii. How mans mind may be joyned with the mind, and Intelligencies of the Celestials, and together with them impress certain wonderfull vertues upon inferiour things.

The Philosophers, especially the Arabians, say, that mans mind, when it is most intent upon any work, through its passion, and effects, is joyned with the mind of the Stars, and Intelligencies, and being so joyned is the cause of some wonderfull vertue be infused into our works, and things; and this, as because there is in it an apprehension, and power of all things, so because all things have a naturall obedience to it, and of necessity an efficacy, and more to that which desires them with a strong desire. And according to this is verified the Art of Characters, images, inchantments [enchantments], and some speeches, and many other wonderfull experiments to every thing which the mind affects. By this means whatsoever the mind of him that is in vehement love affects, hath an efficacy to cause love, & whatsoever the mind of him that strongly hates, dictates, hath an efficacy to hurt, and destroy. The like is in other things, which the mind affects with a strong desire. For all those things which the mind acts, and dictates by Characters, Figures, Words, Speeches, Gestures, and the like, help the appetite of the soul, and acquire certain wonderfull vertues, as from the soul of the operator, in that hour when such a like appetite doth invade it, so from the opportunity, and Celestiall influence, moving the mind in that manner. For our mind, when it is carried upon the great excess of any Passion, or vertue, oftentimes presently takes of it self a strong, better, and more convenient hour, or opportunity. Which Thomas Aquinas in his third book against the Gentiles, confesseth. So many wonderfull vertues both cause, and follow certain admirable operations by great affections, in those things which the soul doth dictate in that hour to them. But know, that such kind of things confer nothing, or very little but to the Author of them, and to him which is inclined to them, as if he were the Author of them. And this is the manner by which their efficacy is found out. And it is a generall rule in them, that every mind that is more excellent in its desire, and affection, makes such like things more fit for it self, as also efficatious to that which it desires. Every one therefore that is willing to work in Magick, must know the vertue, measure, order, and degree of his own soul, in the power of the universe.

Chapter lxviii. How our mind can change, and bind inferiour things to that which it desires.
There is also a certain vertue in the minds of men, of changing, attracting, hindring, and binding to that which they desire, and all things obey them, when they are carried into a great excess of any Passion or vertu [vertue], so as to exceed those things which they bind. For the superior binds that which is inferior, and converts it to it self,

and the inferior is by the same reason converted to the superior, or is otherwise affected, and wrought upon. By this reason things that receive a superior degree of any Star, bind, or attract, or hinder things which have an inferior, according as they agree, or disagree amongst themselves. Whence a Lion is afraid of a Cock, because the presence of the Solary vertue is more agreeable to a Cock then to a Lion: So a Loadstone draws Iron, because in order it hath a superior degree of the Celestiall Bear.

So the Diamond hinders the Loadstone, because in the order of Mars it is superior to it. In like manner any man when he is opportunely exposed to the Celestiall influencies, as by the affections of his mind, so by the due applications of naturall things, if he become stronger in a Solary vertue, binds and draws the inferior into admiration, and obedience, in order of the Moon to servitude or infirmities, in a Saturnall order to quietness or sadness; in order of Jupiter to worship, in order of Mars to fear, and discord, in order of Venus to love, and joy, in a Mercuriall order to perswasion [persuasion], and obsequiousness, and the like. Now the ground of such a kind of binding is the very vehement, and boundless affection of the souls, with the concourse of the Celestiall order. But the dissolutions, or hinderances of such a like binding, are made by a contrary effect, and that more excellent or strong, for as the greater excess of the mind binds, so also it looseth, and hindreth. And lastly, when the [thou] fearest Venus, oppose Saturn. When Saturn or Mars, oppose Venus or Jupiter: for Astrologers say, that these are most at enmity, and contrary the one to the other (i.e.) causing contrary effects in these inferior bodies; For in the heaven, where there is nothing wanting, and where all things are governed with love, there can in no wise be hatred, or enmity.

Chapter lxix. Of Speech, and the vertue of Words.

It being shewed that there is a great power in the affections of the soul, you must know moreover, that there is no less Vertue in words, and the names of things, but greatest of all in speeches, and motions,

by which we chiefly differ from bruits [brutes], and are called rationall; not from reason, which is taken for that part of the soul, which
contains the affections, which Galen saith, is also common to bruits
[brutes], although in a less degree; but we are called rationall, from
that reason which is according to the voice understood in words, and
speech, which is called declarative reason, by which part we do chiefly
excell all other Animals. For λογος [logos] in Greek signifies, reason,
speech, and a word. Now a word is twofold, viz. internall, and uttered; An internall word is a conception of the mind, and motion of
the soul, which is made without a voice. As in dreams we seem to
speak, and dispute with our selves, and whilest we are awake we run
over a whole speech silently. But an uttered word hath a certain act
in the voice, and properties of locution, and is brought forth with the
breath of a man, with opening of his mouth, and with the speech of
his tongue, in which nature hath coupled the corporeall voice, and
speech to the mind, and understanding, making that a declarer, and
interpreter of the conception of our intellect to the hearers, And of
this we now speak. Words therefore are the fittest medium betwixt
the speaker and the hearer, carrying with them not only the conception of the mind, but also the vertue of the speaker with a certain efficacy unto the hearers, and this oftentimes with so great a power, that
oftentimes they change not only the hearers, but also other bodies,
and things that have no life. Now those words are of greater efficacy
then others, which represent greater things, as intellectuall, Celestiall,
and supernaturall, as more expressly, so more misteriously [mysteri-
ously].

Also those that come from a more worthy tongue, or from any of a
more holy order; for these, as it were certain Signs, and representations, receive a power of Celestiall, and supercelestiall things, as from
the vertue of things explained, of which they are the vehicula, so from
a power put into them by the vertue of the speaker.

Chapter lxx. Of the vertue of proper names.

That proper names of things are very necessary in Magicall operations, almost all men testifie: For the naturall power of things proceeds first from the objects to the senses, and then from these to the imagination, and from this to the mind, in which it is first conceived, and then is expressed by voices, and words. The Platonists therefore say, that in this very voice, or word, or name framed, with its Articles, that the power of the thing as it were some kind of life, lies under the form of the signification. First conceived in the mind as it were through certain seeds of things, then by voices or words, as a birth brought forth, and lastly kept in writings. Hence Magicians say, that proper names of things are certain rayes of things, every where present at all times, keeping the power of things, as the essence of the thing signified, rules, and is discerned in them, and know the things by them, as by proper, and living Images. For as the great operator doth produce divers species, and particular things by the influencies of the Heavens, and by the Elements, together with the vertues of Planets; so according to the properties of the influencies proper names result to things, and are put upon them by him who numbers the multitude of the Stars, calling them all by their names, of which names Christ in another place speaks, saying, Your names are written in Heaven. Adam therefore that gave the first names to things, knowing the influencies of the Heavens, and properties of all things, gave them all names according to their natures, as it is written in Genesis, where God brought all things that he had created before Adam, that he should name them, and as he named any thing, so the name of it was, which names indeed contain in them wonderfull powers of the things signified. Every voice therefore that is significative, first of all signifies by the influence of the Celestiall harmony: Secondly, by the imposition of man, although oftentimes otherwise by this, then by that. But when both significations meet in any voice or name, which are put upon them by the said harmony or men, then that name is with a double vertue, viz. naturall, and arbitrary, made most effica-

tious to act, as oft as it shall be uttered in due place, and time, and se-
riously with an intention exercised upon the matter rightly disposed,
and that can naturally be acted upon by it. So we read in Philostratus, that when a maid at Rome dyed [died] the same day she was married, and was presented to Apollonius, he accurately inquired into
her name, which being known, he pronounced some occult thing, by
which she revived. It was an observation amongst the Romanes in
their holy rites, that when they did besiege any City, they did diligently enquire into the proper, and true name of it, and the name of
that God, under whose protection it was, which being known, they
did then with some verse call forth the Gods that were the protectors
of that City, and did curse the inhabitants of that City, so at length
their Gods being absent, did overcome them, as Virgil sings,

- That kept this Realm, our Gods

Their Altars have forsook, and blest abodes.

Now the verse with which the Gods were called out, and the enemies were curst [cursed], when the City was assaulted round about,
let him that would know, finde it out in Livy, and Macrobius; but also
many of these Serenus Samonicus in his book of secret things makes
mention of.

Chapter lxxi. Of many words joyned together, as in sentences, and
verses, and of the vertues, and astrictions of charms.

Besides the vertues of words and names, there is also a greater vertue
found in sentences, from the truth contained in them, which hath a
very great power of impressing, changing, binding, and establishing,
so that being used it doth shine the more, and being resisted is more
confirmed, and consolidated; which vertue is not in simple words, but
in sentences, by which any thing is affirmed, or denyed; of which sort
are verses, enchantments, imprecations, deprecations, orations, invocations, obtestations, adjurations, conjurations, and such like. Therefore in composing verses, and orations, for attracting the vertue of
any Star, or Deity, you must diligently consider what vertues any

Star contains, as also what effects, and operations, and to infer them in verses, by praising, extolling, amplifying, and setting forth those things which such a kind of Star is wont to cause by way of its influence, and by vilifying, and dispraising those things which it is wont to destroy, and hinder, and by supplicating, and begging for that which we desire to get, and by condemning, and detesting that which we would have destroyed, & hindered: and after the same manner to make an elegant oration, and duly distinct by Articles, with competent numbers, and proportions. Moreover Magicians command that we call upon, and pray by the names of the same Star, or name, to them to whom such a verse belongs, by their wonderfull things, or miracles, by their courses, and waies in their sphear [sphere], by their light, by the dignity of their Kingdome, by the beauty, and brightness that is in it, by their strong, and powerfull vertues, and by such like as these. As Psyche in Apuleius prayes to Ceres; saying, I beseech thee by thy fruitfull right hand, I intreat thee by the joyfull Ceremonies of harvests, by the quiet silence of thy chests, by the winged Chariots of Dragons thy servants, by the furrows of the Sicilian earth, the devouring Wagon, the clammy earth, by the place of going down into cellars at the light Nuptials of Proserpina, and returns at the light inventions of her daughter, and other things which are concealed in her temple in the City Eleusis in Attica. Besides, with the divers sorts of the names of the Stars, they command us to call upon them by the names of the Intelligencies, ruling over the Stars themselves, of which we shall speak more at large in their proper place. They that desire further examples of these, let them search into the hymns of Orpheus, then which nothing is more efficatious in naturall Magick, if they together with their circumstances, which wise men know, be used according to a due harmony, with all attention. But to return to our purpose. Such like verses being aptly, and duly made according to the rule of the Stars, and being full of signification, & meaning, and opportunely pronounced with vehement affection, as according to the number, proportion of their Articles, so according to the form resulting from the Articles, and by the violence of imagination, do confer a very great power in the inchanter [enchanter], and sometimes transfers it upon the thing inchanted [enchanted], to bind, and direct it to the same purpose for which the affections, and speeches of the inchanter [enchanter] are intended. Now the instrument of inchanters [enchanters] is a most pure harmoniacall spirit, warm, breathing, living, bringing with it motion, affection, and signification, composed of its parts, endued with sence, and conceived by reason. By the quality therefore of this spirit, and by the Celestiall similitude thereof, besides those things which have already been spoken of, verses also from the opportunity of time, receive from above most excellent vertues, and indeed more sublime, and efficatious then spirits, & vapors exhaling out of the Vegetable life, out of hearbs, roots, gums, aromaticall things, and fumes, and such like. And therefore Magicians inchanting [enchanting] things, are wont to blow, and breath [breathe] upon them the words of the verse, or to breath [breathe] in the vertue with the spirit, that so the whole vertue of the soul be directed to the thing inchanted [enchanted], being disposed for the receiving the said vertue. And here it is to he noted, that every oration, writting [writing], and words, as they induce accustomed motions by their accustomed numbers, and proportions, and form, so also besides their usuall order, being pronounced, or wrote backwards, more unto unusuall effects.

Chapter lxxii. Of the wonderful power of Inchantments [Enchantments].

They say that the power of inchantments [enchantments], and verses is so great, that it is believed they are able to subvert almost all nature, as saith Apuleius, that with a Magicall whispering, swift Rivers are turned back, the slow sea is bound, the Winds are breathed out with one accord, the Sun is stopt, the Moon is clarified, the Stars are pulled out, the day is kept back, the night is prolonged, and of these things sings Lucan,

The courses of all things did cease, the night Prolonged was, 'twas long before 'twas light; Astonied was the headlong world, all this Was by the hearing of a verse ----------

And a little before.

Thessalian verse did into 's heart so flow, That it did make a greater heat of love.

And elsewhere.

No dregs of poison being by him drunk,
His wits decay'd inchanted [enchanted] ----- Also Virgil in Damon. Charms can command the Moon down from the Skie, Circes Charms chang'd Ulisses [Ulysses'] company. A cold Snake being charm'd, burst in the Meads.

And in another place.

charms bear Corn standing from anothers Farm.

And Ovid in his book, sine Titulo, saith.

With charms doth with'ring Ceres dye, Dried are the fountains all, Acorns from Okes [oaks], inchanted [enchanted] Grapes And Apples from trees fall.

If these things were not true, there would not be such strict penall Statutes made against them, that should inchant [enchant] fruit. And Tibullus saith of a certain Imchantress [enchantress],

Her with Charms drawing Stars from Heaven, I And turning th' Course of rivers, did espy,
She parts the earth, and Ghosts from Sepulchers Draws up, and fetcheth bones away from th' fires, And at her pleasure scatters Clouds i'th' Air,
And makes it Snow in Summer hot, and fair.

Of all which that Inchantress [enchantress] seems to boast her self in Ovid, when she saith,

-    At will, I make swift streams retire
To their fountains, whilest their banks admire;
Sea toss, and smooth; clear Clouds, with Clouds deform. With Spells, and Charms I break the Vipers jaw,

Cleave Solid Rocks, Oakes from their seasures [seizures] draw, Whole
Woods remove, the airy Mountains shake,
Earth for to groan, and Ghosts from graves awake, And thee O Moon
I draw -----

Moreover all Poets sing, and Philosophers do not deny, that by
verses many wonderfull things may be done, as Corn to be removed,
Lightenings to be commanded, diseases to be cured, and such like. For
Cato himself in Country affairs used some inchantments [enchant-
ments] against the diseases of beasts, which as yet are extant in his
writings.
Also Josephus testifies that Solomon was skilled in those kinds of inchantments [enchantments]. Also Celsus Africanus reports, according to the Egyptian doctrine, that mans body, according to the
number of the faces of the Zodiack Signs, was taken care of by so
many, viz. thirty six spirits, whereof each undertake, and defend their
proper part, whose names they call with a peculiar voice, which being
called upon, restore to health with their inchantments [enchant-
ments] the diseased parts of the body.

Chapter lxxiii. Of the vertue of writting [writing], and of making
imprecations, and inscriptions.
The use of words, and speech, is to express the inwards of the mind,
and from thence to draw forth the secrets of the thoughts, and to declare the will of the speaker. Now writing is the last expression of the
mind, and is the number of speech and voice, as also the collection,
state, end, continuing, and iteration, making a habit, which is not perfected with the act of ones voice. And whatsoever is in the mind, in
voice, in word, in oration, and in speech, the whole, and all of this is
in writing also. And as nothing which is conceived in the mind is not
expressed by voice, so nothing which is expressed is not also written.
And therefore Magicians command, that in every work, there be imprecations, and inscriptions made, by which the operator may express
his affection: that if he gather an Hearb [herb], or a Stone, he declare

for what use he doth it; if he make a picture, he say, and write to what end he maketh it; with imprecations, and inscriptions. Albertus also in his book called Speculum, doth not disallow, without which all our works would never be brought into effect; Seeing a disposition doth not cause an effect, but the act of the disposition. We find also that the same kind of precepts was in use amongst the Ancients, as Virgil testifies, when he sings,

- I walk a round
First with these threads, in number which three are, 'Bout th' Altars thrice I shall thy Image bear.

And a little after.

Knots, Amaryllis tye [tie]! of Colours three, Then say, these bonds I knit, for Venus be.

And in the same place.

As with one fire this clay doth harder prove, The wax more soft; so Daphnis with our love.

Chapter lxxiv. Of the proportion, correspondency, reduction of Letters to the Celestiall Signs, and Planets, according to various tongues, and a Table shewing this.

God gave to man a mind, and speech, which (as saith Mercurius Trismegistus) are thought to be a gift of the same vertue, power, and immortality. The omnipotent God hath by his providence divided the speech of men into divers languages; which languages have according to their diversity received divers, and proper Characters of writing, consisting in their certain order, number, and figure, not so disposed, and formed by hap, or chance, nor by the weak judgement of man, but from above, whereby they agree with the Celestiall, and divine bodies, and vertues. But before all notes of languages, the writing of the Hebrews is of all the most sacred in the figures of Characters, points of vowels, and tops of accents, as consisting in matter, form, and spirit.

The position of the Stars being first made in the seat of God, which is heaven, after the figure of them (as the masters of the Hebrews testifie) are most fully formed the letters of the Celestiall mysteries, as by their figure, form, and signification, so by the numbers signified by them, and also by their various harmony of their conjunction. Whence the more curious Mecubals of the Hebrews do undertake by the figure of their letters, the forms of Characters, and their signature, simpleness, composition, separation, crookedness, directness, defect, abounding, greatness, litleness, crowning, opening, shutting, order, transmutation, joyning together, revolution of letters, and of points, and tops, by the supputation of numbers by the letters of things signified to explain all things, how they proceed from the first cause, and are again to be reduced into the same. Moreover they divide the letters of their Hebrew Alphabet, viz. into twelve simple, seven double, and three mothers, which they say signifie as Characters of things, the twelve Signs, seven Planets, and three Elements, viz. Fire, Water, and Earth, for they account Aire no Element, but as the glew [glue], and spirit of the Elements. To these also they appoint points, and tops: As therefore by the aspects of Planets, and Signs, together with the Elements, the working spirit, and truth all things have been, and are brought forth, so by these Characters of letters, and points, signifying those things that are brought forth, the names of all things are appointed, as certain Signs, and vehicula's of things explained, carrying with them every where their essence, and vertues. The profound meanings, and Signs are inherent in those Characters, and figures of them, as also numbers, place, order, and revolution; so that Origenes therefore thought that those names being translated into another Idiome, do not retain their proper vertue. For only originall names, which are rightly imposed, because they signify naturally, have a naturall activity: It is not so with them which signifie at pleasure, which have no activity, as they are signifying, but as they are certain naturall things in themselves. Now if there be any originall [language], whose words have a naturall signification, it is manifest that this is the Hebrew, the order of which he that shall profoundly, and radically observe, and shall know to resolve proportionably the letters thereof, shall have a rule exactly to find out any Idiome. There are therefore two and twenty Letters, which are the foundation of the world, and of creatures that are, and are named in it, and every saying, and every creature are of them, and by their revolutions receive their Name, Being, and Vertue.

He therefore that will find them out, must by each joyning together of the Letters so long examine them, untill the voice of God is manifest, and the framing of the most sacred letters be opened, and discovered. For hence voices, and words have efficacy in Magicall works: because that in which nature first exerciseth Magicall efficacy, is the voice of God. But these are of more deep speculation, then to be handled in this book. But to return to the division of the Letters. Of these, amongst the Hebrews, are three mothers, viz., é, å, à; seven double, viz. ú, ø, ô, ë, ã, ð, á. The other 12, viz. ù, ÷,ö,ò, ñ, â, î, ì, è,ç, æ, ä are simple. The same rule is amongst the Chaldeans; And by the imitation of these the letters of other tongues are distributed to Signs, Planets, and Elements, after their order. For the Vowels in the Greek tongue, viz. A E H I O Y Ω answer to the seven Planets. B Γ Δ Z K Λ M N Π P Σ T are attributed to the twelve Signs of the Zodiack, the other five Θ Ξ Φ X Ψ represent the four Elements, and the spirit of the world. Amongst the Latine there is the same signification of them. For the five Vowels A E I 0 U, and J and V Consonants are ascribed to the seven Planets; and the Consonants B C D F G L M N P R S T are answerable to the twelve Signs. The rest, viz. K Q X Z make four Elements. H the aspiration represents the Spirit of the World. Y because it is a Greek, and not a Latine Character, and serving only to Greek words, follows the nature of its Idiome.

But this you must not be ignorant of, that it is observed by all wise men, that the Hebrew letters are the most efficacious of all, because they have the greatest similitude with Celestials, and the world, and that the letters of the other tongues have not so great an efficacy, because they are more distant from them. Now the disposition of these, the following Table will explain. Also all the Letters have double numbers of their order, viz. Extended, which simply express of what number the letters are, according to their order: and collected, which recollect with themselves the numbers of all the preceding letters.

Also they have integrall numbers, which result from the names of Letters, according to their various manners of numbring [numbering]. The vertues of which numbers, he that shall know, shall be able in every tongue to draw forth wonderfull mysteries by their letters, as also to tell what things have been past, and foretell things to come. There are also other mysterious joynings of letters with numbers: but we shall abundantly discourse of all these in the following Books: Wherefore we will now put an end to this first Book.

9 781998 614806